A PRACTIONER'S GUIDE

THE FUNDAMENTALS OF SCHOOL SOCIAL WORK

WITH

CAVEMAN WISDOM ABOUT BECOMING A SCHOOL SOCIAL WORKER

Dr. Raymond D. McCoy, Jr, MSW, Psy.D.
LCSW, LCP, SSW (Retired)
Copyright: 09/01/2017
Reg.# TXu 2-046-844

TABLE OF Contents:

CHAPTERS:

CHAPTER 1

SOCIAL WORK, PSYCHOLOGY, AND SCHOOL SOCIAL WORK COMPARED AND CONTRASTED:

CHAPTER 2

THE FUNDAMENTALS OF (REAL) SCHOOL SOCIAL WORK

CHAPTER 3

CHAPTER 4

CHAPTER 5

CHAPTER 6

CHAPTER 7

1-ASD Screening
2- Diagnostic Criteria for Asperger's Disorder
3-Section 504 of the ADA Amendments Act of 2008
4-What to Consider Before Determining if a Student Is Eligible
    for IDEA and/or 504 Services
5-Birth Weight and the Implications of Low Birth Weight
6-Childhood Onset Bipolar Disorder
7-Visual Processing Disorder
8-Auditory Processing Disorder
9-Sequential Processing Disorder
10-Conceptual/Holistic Processing Disorder

TO THE READERS OF THIS GUIDEBOOK

My goal in writing **A PRACTITIONER'S GUIDE: THE FUNDAMENTALS OF SCHOOL SOCIAL WORK with CAVEMAN WISDOM ABOUT BECOMING A SCHOOL SOCIAL WORKER,** is to make this book not only informative, but practical and useful to the School Social Worker practitioner, and hopefully, a bit humorous as well. Life is too short to skip the humor, and research tells us that we learn better when we experience positive emotions.

I use the terms **Caveman and Wisdom** together, (although some might say it is an oxymoron), to describe humans as consummate survivors, always learning new ways to adapt and change to their environment.

I am hoping that my **Caveman Wisdoms** may be just what you need to survive and thrive as you perform the duties of a School Social Worker. I will also be making many *–"Look it up"* comments when I know there is relevant research easily found on the internet that you should quickly look up and read and become familiar with.

We learn new information by cognitively "processing" information through **assimilation** and **accommodation.** We also learn and adapt from our mistakes. We do this by creating new perceptions and cognitive ideas or **(schemas).** We call that **adaptation,** and adaptation is a form of higher learning and is needed to survive whether you are running away from a T-Rex or managing the complexities of a bureaucratic school system and/or social work services and school policies.

As you can see, I will be referring to *Piaget's theory of learning frequently; i.e. SCHEMA, ORGANIZATION, ASSIMMILATION, ACCOMMODATION, AND ADAPTATION-(look it up).*

When I mark certain statements from time to time with **"CAVEMAN WISDOM",** this will denote a famous quote with words of wisdom and/or a practical social work related anecdotes based on my professional experience.

School Social Work is a complex type of Social Work. In practice it contains professional elements from many different social, educational, and psychological fields of study; i.e. Clinical Social Work, Clinical Psychology, Child Development, Pediatric Neurology, Child and Adolescent Psychiatry, Education, Educational Law, Juvenile and Domestic Court Law, and Family Relationships to name a few. There are probably many more that you can and will think of.

These varied professional domains encompass the fundamental framework of "school social work services".

The variety of different professional domains and coursework is not typically mentioned or customarily taught in a school social work curriculum/specialization track; but I am here to tell you that aspects of these multi-disciplinary professions is what school social work will focus on in your day to day practice.

The School Social Worker, hence forward, referred to as (SSW), interacts with a cross section of humanity. You will be evaluating and providing social work interventions to a wide range of children, and their parents, who will manifest a wide range of normal, and abnormal, personalities, socio-economic differences, medical illnesses, psychological disorders, and learning disabilities. You will see and hear it all; well, most of it anyway.

You will make mistakes during your career; it is a fact of life. Mistakes can be good for you, as long as they are not **major** work related ethical or competency quagmires that gobble you up in bureaucratic politics or professional conflicts. These can be quite nasty and difficult to recover from, so beware. Otherwise making most other types of work related mistakes teaches you what doesn't work so well, and how to get it right! Our many mistakes are an essential part of our personal and professional development. Because we humans have developed a rather profound "Pre-Frontal Cerebral Cortex" over the millennia, we can also learn from other people's mistakes just as well, and become just as successful, with a minimal number of direct personal mistakes to suffer through. I refer to this process of learning as **CAVEMAN WISDOM**.

CAVEMAN WISDOM: "The only man who never makes a mistake is the man who never does anything". By: Theodore Roosevelt.

CAVEMAN WISDOM : "No man was ever so completely skilled in the conduct of life, as not to receive new information from age and experience". By: Terence.

TRIVIA QUESTION:

Do you know why they named the popular spray found in most garages and households **WD-40?** WD-40 is a **W**ater **D**isplacement spray, (not a lubricating oil). It took **40** attempts at manufacturing it to get it right. Hence WD-40.

What if they had given up on trial number 39 saying; hey, we've made way too many mistakes, let's forget about this already? Because they kept making mistakes, and because they kept learning something new, in the end, they were successful. They created WD-40. Someone is certainly a multi-millionaire!

Use **CAVEMAN WISDOM** and learn from me; my mistakes and my successes can hopefully become your vicarious learning experiences. You will then have an opportunity to cognitively **ORGANIZE** new ideas and valuable information about School Social Work. It will help you to begin to form your own **SCHEMAS**, process your own **ASSIMMILATIONS** and make your own A**COMMODATIONS**, ultimately leading to personal **ADAPTATIONS** without the pain and embarrassment of making too many personal mistakes on the job.

If you are already working, whoops, I'm too late. You have already made some mistakes, but hopefully you have also had the good fortune to assimilate, accommodate, and adapt.

CAVEMAN WISDOM: "Failure is the opportunity to begin again more intelligently".
By: Moshe Arens.

DEDICATION:
Learn to Survive and Thrive On the Job

The author is a retired Licensed Clinical Psychologist, Licensed Clinical Social Worker, and Professional School Social Worker with 43 years of combined work experience. This book is written as much to inform you, as it is to motivate you. Humor is, in my humble opinion, loved by everyone, and a useful tool that humans have used for several years (humor) to survive the stresses of life; so this book is also written in a somewhat "humorous" tone, as it is my belief that you must maintain a sense of humor in life if you are to survive and thrive.

I know what it is like to be a Social Worker, a Psychologist, and a School Social Worker, as well as a few other things in life. I've done what you are doing. I was a School Social Worker for 21 years. It was the second largest school system in the state. Our department had 35 SSWs working full time. We were assigned to approximately three different schools. There was no vertical ladder for promotion in the SSW department. You got up every morning doing the same thing day in and day out, just hoping to retire with some sense of sanity (and a retirement pension).

Most social workers say they enjoy their jobs because they are helping others. Even so, most jobs have more similarities than differences. Work is difficult. Any and all jobs are stressful and stress can take a huge psychological toll. Add the WORK stress to the LIFE stress and you've got a full plate. Life is very stressful, whether you are married, or not married. Parenting children and a maintaining a full time job is just plain horrific! Personal relationships and work-place relationships are complicated and most always a bit difficult; and sometimes, very, very difficult! Stress can occur either from your clients' troubles, your extremely difficult co-workers, or a %$*&@ boss!

We've all been there. It is life. It must be dealt with and overcome. You must learn to assimilate, accommodate, and adapt in order to survive, and then thrive, if you want that retirement pension; and oh yes, your sanity. That's important too!

What I quickly learned was how to **adapt** to the job while on the job. My choice was to constantly **grow professionally** while on the job, or hate the job and become stagnate and unhappy. This helped me actually **learn how to enjoy the job**. This required that I **"reinvent"** myself as a School Social Worker, and change my perspective about my **professional identity**.

CAVEMAN WISDOM: "The measure of intelligence is the ability to change." **Albert Einstein**

I adapted to the job as a School Social Worker during my 21 years in order to thrive, and so can you. I was already an LCSW when I was hired as an SSW with 20 years of prior social work experience, but it was unrelated to **school** social work experience. So naturally, my school district felt is was only fair to not compensate me for any prior experience or LCSW credentials!

The fact of the matter is, all your prior jobs, all that previous training and your clinical certifications/clinical licensures that you earn **prior to becoming an SSW** does make you a much better SSW than if you just graduated from that MSW degree program with an SSW track. Experience is the golden teacher.

CAVEMAN WISDOM: "Forgive, Adapt and Evolve, because holding on stagnates your opportunity of being better. By: Sachin Kumar Puli

School social work is not just about kids in school getting an education and having learning problems; it is also about kids who are in the social welfare system, living in homeless families, kids in the juvenile justice system experiencing delinquency issues, kids with mental illness who have parents with mental health problems, living in severely dysfunctional families and poverty, kids abusing drugs, kids bullying others and being bullied, kids being violent and aggressive, etc, etc. .

School is a complex social system that integrates the surrounding community and culture, not the other way around. A formal education might be seen as an artificial learning experience and process that takes place in a separate school facility, impacted heavily either positively or negatively by those that reside in that child's complex socio-cultural environment.

In order for me to thrive and stay alive during my 21-year SSW career, I earned a Psy.D. in Clinical Psychology (on-line program) while working as a full time School Social Worker and part time LCSW in private practice. Earning that Psy.D. and getting licensed as a Clinical Psychologist at age 53 was a goal I had put on hold for 20 years after I had started a Ph.D. program previously and completed 20 hours as a Ph.D. candidate in Child Development. It ultimately enhanced my clinical acumen as a School Social Worker tremendously.

An SSW with a Ph.D./Psy.D. in Clinical Psychology still has to remember that they are working as a **School Social Worker, and not a School Psychologist.** Your job description defines your ethical and professional job parameters, not your educational degrees! Don't let it bother you though.

An MSW/SSW has it over a School Psychologist any day in my opinion. When you know how boring it can get to give IQ and achievement tests over and over and over, day in and day out, you realize how lucky you are to be the School Social Worker! What is quite helpful though during those parent interviews, SEC meetings and 504 meetings, is that you know what an IQ test and achievement test really says about a student, and what they don't say and can't possibly say about a student's full human potential.

As a School Social Worker, a good social and developmental history, done right, says more about a student's life potential than any IQ test or achievement test.

CAVEMAN WISDOM: "Because IQ tests favor memory skills and logic, overlooking artistic creativity, insight, resiliency, emotional reserves, sensory gifts, and life experience, they can't really predict success, let alone satisfaction." By: Diane Ackerman, An Alchemy of Mind: The Marvel and Mystery of the Brain.

CAVEMAN WISDOM: "Learning can never be quantified with a flawed educational unit."
By: Louise Philippe Dulay.

CAVEMAN WISDOM: "Intelligence is the ability to adapt to change". Stephen Hawking

Someone who is *CREATIVE* means they are **inventive and productive**; they create something new and original. They develop new ideas and new ways of thinking about something old, and put them into practice in a new and original way. Being creative also means you learn to adapt to the old and mundane circumstances, as well as new and different circumstances.

If you want to last 20+ years as an SSW *you must be creative* in order to survive that long without going bonkers and professionally acting like a comatose manikin. It happens. Those comatose people are all around you as we speak; just turn around and look at some of your fellow colleagues who have been on the job for more than 10 years. Am I right! Yes! You know I am! What is their primary occupational interest; probably where they will go to lunch, right! Do they disappear for hours and no one really knows where they are? Do they have a sarcastic/negative attitude and just get by, doing the very minimum? They may have become mere robots, operating in a daze, complaining everyday about the job and the people they serve. They have fallen in the quagmire and/or are burnt out.

Change in one's **job perception** often results in various degrees of change to our **self-confidence, professional competency, and occupational motivation.**

CAVEMAN WISDOM: "Human beings, who are almost unique in having the ability to learn from the experience of others, are also remarkable for their apparent disinclination to do so!".
By: Douglas Noel Adams.

I have developed my own theory of job satisfaction and professional competence. I believe that there is a spectrum of personal and professional job satisfaction that develops when someone works too long at only one job. It seems to me that after 5 years of doing the same thing, something changes in our view about the job, whatever that job might be.

My "**Jobology Framework**", (i.e. not a professional term!), was derived by studying my own levels of job satisfaction from the inside out. I worked (5) different jobs over a 22-year period **before** becoming a School Social Worker, and then worked in that job for 21 years straight. My perception of job satisfaction tends to fall **into three basic phases: 1)-Dedication; 2)-Determination; and 3)-Desperation.**

-Dedication- (Dictionary definition-the quality of being dedicated or committed to a task or purpose)

This is usually seen during the first 1 to 5 years on the job. You still feel highly educated and motivated with a sense of self-confidence and professional competence. You are ready to take on the world and be the best SSW there ever was. You go to great CE workshops and always feel energized with a renewed sense of professional acumen on the job.

During the first 5 years or so of a new job, we are excited. Why? Because we are employed for one thing; and because we are learning something new, we are challenged. We are **DEDICATED, or committed,** to the job and the career path we have chosen. We tend to perform well during this period with a high degree of job satisfaction, self-confidence, and competency. We feel energized and confident that we can use our newly formulated MSW research tricks and therapeutic modalities and interventions to help others. Isn't it wonderful! Another day in paradise!

-DETERMINATION: (Dictionary definition-a fixed purpose or intention; a fixed direction or tendency toward some object or end) (e.g. retirement!)

The employee has been on the job more than 5 years but less than 15 years. Work has become a routine. You know what it is all about and no longer feel professionally challenged. You wonder if there is something more you could do to feel more professionally worthwhile. Your sense of **professional competence is getting stale**. You are no longer interested in paying out of pocket for your own CEUs because you feel **the system OWES YOU** at least that much, so you haven't been to a worthwhile CE workshop in years. Now you only go to the departmental FLUFF that is offered for free. Now you no longer value continuing education as a professional growth mainstay, but rather as a departmental requirement that you now dread.

As the years pass by, and you are now into your 10-15 year mark, you are no longer "excited" when you get that beautiful coffee cup with the institutional logo and an official certificate with "Congratulations on your 10th year" Employee. You may even feel used and abused. Maybe over worked or even underworked. No one any longer respects your professional competency because you are stale and you are stuck in a rut. You haven't learned anything new since you graduated 15 years ago. (By now, all the research you learned in grad school is so old it is no longer professionally relevant).

But, more important, those MSW intervention techniques you used to feel so good about are now outdated, and/or ineffective, and there are newer therapeutic modalities and new research based theories and interventions out there, but you kind of "don't care". You tell yourself that your MSW is all you need to succeed, right!

Knowing something about the new research on childhood bipolar disorder and/or temperament dysregulation disorder, for instance, and how separation anxiety can transform into social anxiety and that can escalate into school phobia, might actually help the SSW understand the nature of how school refusal behavior develops in many children, but you kind of just don't care anymore.

And to add insult to injury, there is no pat on the back? No job well done from teachers, supervisors and administrators? Instead it sounds, and feels, more like... "Congratulations, **you've somehow managed to last 10-15 years on the job** Mr./Mrs. School System Employee....".

You might admit to yourself, if you take a moment to honestly reflect, that you do indeed feel professionally stagnate, but **DETERMINED** to hang in there for the benefits until retirement. You are almost at the half way mark. That's what the congratulations is about, you are half way to retirement! It isn't about how well you perform your job.

Have you been keeping up with the newest research? Do you still enjoy going to continuing education workshops or are you stuck in the past still reciting 1980s, 1990s, 2000's research; when was the year you earned your MSW? If you are not educationally relevant, you can't be professionally competent!

CAVEMAN WISDOM: "The man who views the world at 50 the same as he did at 20 has wasted 30 years of his life". By: Mohammad Ali.

You tell yourself, at night, in your hypnogogic dream state, that your strong sense of commitment and determination has always been one of your strengths; that you are smart and went to a good University or College and did very well; so what is the problem? The problem is that your professional determination has transformed into occupational desolation!

You have always been a competent Social Worker, at least during the first 5 years of those 10-15 years on the job anyway. But you continue to say to yourself, what else is there? There is no way I can go back to school and work and balance my family life! There is nowhere to go, no vertical promotional opportunities, and only more of the same old stuff, different day but same routine. If you now feel stuck, and only go to work so you can get to 30 years and retire, you are in professional trouble.

You also begin to realize that you are now really, really tired of getting up so early in the morning. But you must keep going. You must complete 15-20 more years to get to retirement. You are only at the half way mark! You need your benefit package and pension. Please, somebody, help me! This is when we become *DESPERATE*; **phase** 3 of my "Jobology Framework". **Desperation is dangerous to any career.**

CAVEMAN WISDOM: "Disappointment should always be taken as a stimulant, and never viewed as a discouragement". By: C.B. Newcomb.

CAVEMAN WISDOM: "Desperation is sometimes as powerful an inspirer as is genius". By: Benjamin Desraeli.

-**DESPERATION**-(Dictionary definition-A state of despair, typically one that results in rash or extreme behavior. Loss of hope, state of hopelessness).

So, you are a seasoned School Social Worker with more than 15 years of experience, but you feel professionally stale and maybe even a bit bitter that the "system" hasn't been better to you; no promotions are available; you get no raises (that really count); and there have been no job related changes in your duties or responsibilities to the day-in and day-out hum drum routine for over 15-20 years. You begin to think that this job is killing you; your creativity and your intellect are being wasted, but there is nothing else for you to do in the "educational bureaucracy". **DESPERATION** sets in. A sense of professional hopelessness is becoming pervasive. Maybe you are even clinically depressed.

You are approaching "**professional despair**". You wonder how in the world you will ever last another 10 or 15 years until retirement. You realize your kids are going to college in a few years and if you want a pension, you have to stick it out.

What do you do to thrive and survive for the duration?

CAVEMAN WISDOM: "My father taught me to work; he did not teach me to love it". By: Lincoln.

Now, focus. Do you remember what the clinician's definition of insanity is: "doing the same thing over and over, but expecting different results". Don't go insane. Don't get stuck doing the same thing day in and day out expecting different results.

CAVEMAN WISDOM: "You've achieved success in your field when you don't know whether what you are doing is work or play". By: Warren Beatty.

Start to work on your renewed sense of professional development and turn it into a renewed sense of self-confidence; via enhanced professional competency, and ultimately, a heightened personal and professional identity.

Don't just do whatever the minimum numbers of required CEUs are that the school system requires you to complete. Think how you can develop your professional skills and learn something new for you, not for them!

Develop a professional specialty; be the best at understanding something, (i.e. truancy; childhood emotional disorders; the 504 law, Asperger's disorder, ADHD, OCD, etc.) Pick one; there are plenty to choose from. Read, study, and learn. Repeat.

Assimilate, Accommodate, Adapt!

Work on your LCSW or M.Ed., Ph.D., or Psy.D. Get an "Educational Specialist" certification (30 hours of course work beyond the Masters degree). Take an evening college course. Take **interesting continuing education courses**, not just that personal development stuff that your school division offers and/or requires, and don't even think about counting that free 90 CEU hour college course your division offers i.e. "Curriculum Development" from the local University; just because it is EASY and it is FREE, It is not INTERESTING, it is not conducive to School Social Work job competency, and it will not reward you personally or professionally.

What is your professional identity? What do you want your professional competency, within the field of School Social Work, to be, and to say about you as an SSW? Pursue it. Enjoy learning something new and important to you and the populations that your serve. That MSW and Professional School Social Work licensure is just the beginning layer of a professional identity, not the culmination.

Take CEU courses that mean something to you personally and professionally and that will ultimately make you a better social worker. **Check out CE-CREDIT.com; crosscountryeducation.com; PESI.com; and zurinstitute.com.** These are just a few of the **continuing education programs you can access online** that offer workshops in a location near you, and/or internet-based CEU courses and certifications for social workers and psychologists.

There are many interesting CEU courses out there that are relevant to todays SSW: **"DSM-5, Friend or Foe"; "Brain-Based Therapy and Practical Neuroscience: Attachment and Emotional Regulation"; "Social Difficulties of Learning: Attentional and Autism Spectrum Disorders: Screening and Treatment"; "Assessment of Children: Behavioral and Clinical Applications"; "The Explosive Child"; "The Many Faces of Anxiety in Children and Adolescents", and "A Best Practice Guide to Assessment and Intervention for Autism and Asperger's Syndrome in Schools".**

And there are literally thousands more to choose from. This type of continuing education can actually help you grow as a professional and a School Social Worker. Think about being in an SEC meeting. Who are the experts? The Teacher is the educational expert. The School Psychologist is one; and you are too, believe it or not, so act like an expert! Get smart (not the TV guy) learn something new and be the expert who knows about cutting edge research that can help a child in need reach their potential.

During an SEC meeting, or a parent interview, when you are discussing a child who exhibits symptoms of a learning problem, can you competently discuss the side effects of his asthma medications, his high level of frustration because of an undiagnosed learning disability, ADHD, or anxiety issues? Do you know how his/her chronic sleep deprivation affects their learning?

Is there a chronic history of atypical separation anxiety and/or shy temperament that impedes social relationships and learning style? Is that child's chronic sleepiness in class from insomnia, or an absence seizure disorder that has been contributing to the student's learning problems?

All of these conditions' and symptoms look like ADHD. If you have become knowledgeable about these issues, through reading good research or going to good CEU workshops, you will be armed with professionally competent information that provides you with the clinical **acumen** (look it up) that can help you assist the SEC team and the child's parents unravel the student's learning problems. Your social history interview with the student's parent(s) can uncover all of these conditions if you know what to look for and how to ask the right questions.

CAVEMAN WISDOM: "Knowledge will bring you the opportunity to make a difference".
By: Claire Fagin

You have now become an expert, congratulations! Your enhanced clinical acumen, derived from years of education, experience and first rate CEU courses, will now contribute to a first rate social history assessment. It will be much appreciated, and very informative, for the parents, and teachers alike. The parents of the student you are screening and/or evaluating will finally have a possible answer to their child's dilemma. You can now plan appropriate educational and/or SSW home and school based interventions.

If you are feeling professionally stagnate, shake it up, learn something new, and do something new and exciting for your schools, teachers, parents and students. Develop a group for the parents with children who have emotional disorders and discuss parenting and coping techniques and strategies. Bring in guest speakers who are local specialists. Run an anger management group for students. Run a group for parents of children who manifest school refusal/school anxiety issues. (Not for the students though, they won't come!)

Develop and write an **e-mail newsletter for teachers and parents** about various topics: i.e., school social work services; fighting; truancy; bulling; strategies for coping with a child with severe ADHD or an emotional disorder; or something else that Teachers and/or parents can use in their daily lives.

The job is what you make it, so make it exciting and fun and do good stuff for people!
You can proceed along the SSW road at 30 miles per hour for 30 years and learn nothing new

and do nothing new. Or, you can jump start a new chapter in your career at 65 miles per hour and feel energized, competent, and self-confident.

CAVEMAN WISDOM: Whenever you are *asked if you can do a job, tell them, Certainly, I can! Then get busy and find out how to do it. By: Theodore Roosevelt*

CAVEMAN WISDOM: The biggest mistake that you can make is to believe that you are working for somebody else…The driving force of a career must come from the individual. Remember: **Jobs are owned by the company**, but **you own your career**! – By: Earl Nightingale

INTRODUCTION:

Learning how to perform the official duties and responsibilities of the School Social Worker competently, or any profession for that matter, requires **education**, **specialized training** and **experience**. It also requires that you **learn to continuously adapt to relevant new research**.

What are the fundamental domains of School Social Work? Is this a profession that mostly identifies with Social Work, Psychology, or Education? Does it require clinical skills, administrative skills, or teaching skills?

I will be, and have been, harping on professional growth and adapting to the job in order to survive and thrive. So what do I mean by professional ADAPTATION? Here is the simple version I find most relevant according to *Piaget's learning theory*:

1) **STEP ONE**- The **Organization** of one's learning experiences. *("Executive Functioning Skills" might be very important to this stage-look it up).*
2) **STEP TWO**-The **Assimilation** of new ideas, the process of incorporating new information i.e., professional research, into your old perceptions or (*schemas-look it up*);
3) **STEP THREE**-Then, hopefully, **Accommodation will** occur, which is the questioning and cognitive reflection upon the old *schemas* (previously learned information) and the active modification of one's perceptions; which hopefully, for all mankind, and all School Social Workers, will lead to the final learning stage.
4) **STEP FOUR**-**Adaptation**, which is the **internalized** adjustment of previously learned Information (cognitive ideas) into a **new schema** (new and better cognitive perceptions and ideas).

Earning an MSW is just the first building block. Then you must continue to study and learn; Assimilate (more). Accommodate (more). Then you can adapt. Study/Learn. REPEAT. Become a CAVEMAN. Cavemen had to learn to be WISE in order to survive. . Develop **CAVEMAN WISDOM** and really learn how to enjoy your work and excel at your profession.

I have already sung the praises for continuing education, in any form. The Internet makes reading new research very easy. Make it a habit to read at least two articles a day. Print them and save them. Organize and keep them in reading files and then read them again before giving them to someone else. Don't ever throw them away. Summarize what you have learned and put it into your "SSW e-mail Newsletter" that you send to colleagues or discuss over a brown bag lunch hour with colleagues. Many programs allow this to be considered as CEU/Professional Development hours, if approved beforehand. School Social Work is a great profession. It can be very rewarding. You just need to learn how to make it work for you, as much as you work for it.

CAVEMAN WISDOM: "Education is the path from cocky ignorance to miserable uncertainty".
By: Mark Twain.

CAVEMAN WISDOM: "Wisdom is not a product of schooling, but a lifelong attempt to acquire it". By: Albert Einstein

CHAPTER 1:

SOCIAL WORK, PSYCHOLOGY, AND SCHOOL SOCIAL WORK COMPARED AND CONTRASTED:

I miss going to the University library to look something up. So many books. That book smell. That heavy book feel. Most University libraries are huge. There is a unique "academic feeling" associated with entering a University library. It is a good feeling. It makes you believe that you are about to learn something new and important.

However, many times the book I was told to read was missing or checked out. Not so if you look it up on the Internet. Now, turn your computer on and visit one of your favorite Internet search engines and enter a search word or idea. Look up ADHD, or the 504 law, or school social work services, for instance. In seconds there is literally a list of thousands of web sites to click on to get your answer.

Here is a compilation of professional definitions that I found in my brief search on the Internet:

(1). SOCIAL WORK DEFINED:

Social Work is the work carried out by trained personnel with the aim of alleviating the conditions of those in need of help or welfare.

The professional activity of helping individuals, groups, or communities enhance or restore their capacity for social functioning and creating societal conditions favorable to this goal.

The professional activity aimed at enhancing problem solving, coping, and the developmental capacities of people.

The professional activity to promote the effective and humane operation of the systems that provide people with resources and services.

Organized work intended to advance the social conditions of a community, and especially of the disadvantaged, by providing psychological counseling, guidance, and assistance, especially in the form of social services.

(2). <u>SCHOOL SOCIAL WORK (SSW) DEFINED:</u>

The School Social Worker is an advocate who helps students reach their potential in the educational setting by providing support services in order to remove obstacles to a child's success in school.

The School Social Work profession has consistently focused on coordinating the efforts of schools, families, and communities toward helping students improve their academic achievement and social, emotional, and behavioral competence by using its unique perspective of viewing the person in his or her environment.

School Social Workers are one of the three professional pupil services groups that provide counseling services to children and adolescents in schools, structured around expanding practice models: the traditional clinical model; the school change model; the community school model: and the social interaction model... in order to work with students and their parents regarding social and emotional difficulties.

School Social Work is a specific field of social work practice, and encompasses the main areas of social work practice within educational settings, providing: direct practice, service management, organizational development and system change, policy, research, and educational and professional development.

School Social Workers are one of the three professional pupil services groups that provide counseling services to children and adolescents in schools in the United States. School Social Workers have worked in schools for over 100 years and are recognized in a majority of U.S. states and several foreign countries. Most School Social Workers hold a Master of Social Work degree and have specialized training in helping students within the context of local schools.

At its inception, School Social Workers were known, among other things, as advocates for equity and fairness as well as home visitors. The expansion of School Social Work services was encouraged by a number of factors. By 1900 over two-thirds of the states had compulsory attendance laws and by 1918, each state had passed compulsory attendance laws, making school attendance obligatory, and not simply a privilege.

From 1940-1960 casework in schools had become an established specialty, the profession began to emphasize collaboration and communication with teachers and other school personnel. Now the School Social Worker is considered an expert who can help schools with psychosocial issues.

(3). PSYCHOLOGY DEFINED:

The scientific study of the human mind and its functions, especially those affecting behavior in a given context.

The study of the mind and behavior, from the functions of the brain to the actions of nations, from child development to the care for the aged.

The science that deals with mental processes and behavior; the emotional and behavioral characteristics of an individual, group, or activity.

The branch of metaphysics that studies the soul, the mind, and the relationship of life and the mind to the functions of the body.

The scientific study of all forms of human and animal behavior sometimes concerned with the methods through which behavior can be modified.

The purpose of psychology is to give us a completely different idea of the things that we know best.

(4). SCHOOL PSYCHOLOGIST (SP) DEFINED:

The APA defines SP as: a general practice and health service provider specialty of professional psychology that is concerned with the science and practice of psychology with children, youth, families; learners of all ages; and the schooling process.

The basic education and training of school psychologists prepares them to provide a range of psychological diagnosis, assessment, intervention, prevention, health promotion, and program development and evaluation services with a special focus on the developmental processes of children and youth within the context of schools, families and other systems.

SP is a discipline that employs concepts of clinical psychology and academic psychology to the analysis and therapy for children and adolescents' behavioral and educational issues.

Campus psychologists are qualified in psychology, child and adolescent growth, child and adolescent psychopathology, education and learning, family unit and parenting techniques, education concepts, and character philosophies. School psychologists are uniquely qualified members of school teams that support students' ability to learn and teachers' ability to teach. They apply expertise in mental health, learning, and behavior, to help children and youth succeed academically, socially, behaviorally, and emotionally.

School psychologists partner with families, teachers, school administrators, and other professionals to create safe, healthy, and supportive learning environments that strengthen connections between home, school, and the community.

School psychologists receive specialized advanced graduate preparation that includes coursework and practical experiences relevant to both psychology and education, with emphasis in data collection and analysis; intellectual assessment; behavioral monitoring; consultation and collaboration; mental health intervention; special education services; crisis preparedness, response, and recovery.

CAVEMAN WISDOM: Do you see any glaring differences between the definitions regarding the practice of Social Work, Psychology, and School Social Work? Do you see any similarities?

SUMMARY:

There are definite differences noted by me in these definitions, however, having practiced as a Licensed Clinical Social Worker, a Licensed Clinical Psychologist, and a Professioinal School Social Worker, there are many more similarities in real life practice, than there are differences.

What Social Workers don't do that Clinicl Psychologists and School Psychologists do, however, is administer IQ tests, Achievement tests, personality tests, and a variety of other standardized psychometric instruments. No matter what level of experience you may have, social workers are usually deemed by professional ethics and practice parameters, to not be professionally qualified to administer these types of psychometric tests without further education, training and/or certification in psychology.

This does not mean that a School Social Worker should not study these tests. While you may never get your hands on an actual Wechsler IQ test kit, you should read a good book about **child and adolescent psychological assessment** and understand what these tests can and can't do, and what the results mean when they are read to you at the SEC or 504 committee meeting.

You need to understand and become very familiar with raw scores, percentiles, stanine scores, standard scores, the bell curve, IQ ranges, achievement scores, and behavior rating scale scores.

While these tests can be informative, they provide no magic answers. Usually they just validate what the teacher and parents have been saying about the student for months or years! They are, in reality, very simple to administer and score. (It used to be common place many years ago that anyone with a B.S. in Psychology could become a Psychometrist and administer any and all psychological tests under the supervision of a Ph.D. Psychologist). The clinical interpretation of the test results is what takes a good deal of training and experience to get good at; i.e., a score or a profile can mean something different when applied in different contexts and when compared to individually specific bio-psycho-social backgrounds.

Cook-book interpretations are dangerous and usually do more harm than good to the individual being evaluated.

CAVEMAN WISDOM: "A wonderful fact to reflect upon, that every human creature is constituted to be that profound secret and mystery to every other." By: Charles Dickens.

Psychological tests mainly provide us with a "good idea" of a student's cognitive strengths and weaknesses. It tends to "predict the potential for academic success". These tests cannot foretell the future, contrary to popular belief. Social, emotional, and developmental issues play a big part in fully understanding an individual's cognitive, psychological and human potential. And a person's (human) potential is not decided by an IQ score at any age; even at that majic age of (8), when everyone was told by the School Psychologist to wait until they are in the 3rd grade and the results are felt to be more valid.

Some children's cognitive skills develop more slowly and inconsistently. While most Psychologists/School Psychologists might repeat the often cited, and politically correct theory, that "IQ scores remain fairly consistent from around the age of 7 or 8 and upward", I have seen many situations that did not reflect this doctrine, and to **assume** so, is not always in the best interest of every child.

CAVEMAN WISDOM: "In theory, theory and practice are the same. In practice, they are not". By: Yogi Berra.

The brain is a very complex organ and cannot be reduced to an IQ score alone. In parts of California the use of IQ scores to determine eligibility for special education services has been eliminated in some situations, and is not permitted to be part of the assessment process.(**Look it up).**

"Because of the Larry P. v. Riles case, the California State Department of Education (CDE) has prohibited school districts from using standardized IQ tests to determine special education eligibility for all African-American students. Therefore, school districts are developing alternative methods of assessment to avoid the use of IQ scores for special education eligibility determination".

Remember, one of the SSW's most important roles in the comprehensive assessment process is to evaluate a student's **adaptive behavior. "**Social competence, or adaptive behavior, refers to the progressive development or maturation of the human organism...adaptive behavior can be quantified by sampling representative performance at successive age levels".

The measurement of adaptive behavior differs from measures of intelligence in that it samples actual day-to-day performance of basic living skills rather than innate or perceived intellectual or academic abilities"; i.e. which tend to be somewhat arbitrarily limited by the educational/academic curriculum, and theoretical definitions of intelligence, which there are many! **(look it up-define intelligence).**

Sometimes adaptive behavior is more revealing than any IQ score, so don't count your job as a School Social Worker any less important than the School Psychologist. Get good at assessing adaptive behavior. Become an expert. Make your report count, and make it mean just as much as the School Psychology report.

Report the student's many strengths and talents, as well as weaknesses. Utilize the positive attribution/strength based approach, not just the negative attribution or deficit approach. Children are entitled to be considered as a whole, and not just broken down into various parts or scores from a test.

CAVEMAN WISDOM: "Psychology keeps trying to vindicate human nature. History keeps undermining the effort". By: Mason Cooley.

CAVEMAN WISDOM: "If you want your children to be intelligent, read them fairy tales. If you want them to be more intelligent, read them more fairy tales." By: **Albert Einstein**

CHAPTER 2

THE FUNDAMENTALS OF (REAL) SCHOOL SOCIAL WORK:

This book is intended to be used as a professional manual and SSW guide. I will cite research and theoretical constructs in order to provide the reader with examples of good practice. My intent is to provide the reader with a realistic and anecdotal perspective on the "real life duties and responsibilities of a School Social Worker" that I have personally and professionally come to know.

What are the qualifications of a School Social Worker? While every school district does "their own thing", some "things" are "supposed" to have "standard operating procedures". **To be a School Social Worker, you are "supposed to" have a Master Degree in Social Work (MSW) with specialization in School Social Work.** There are some older versions of School Social Work services called "Visiting Teachers" that used to allow the professional to have an MA, MS or M.Ed. instead of a graduate Social Work degree; but in general, not a BSW, BS or BA degree.

If you don't have your MSW yet, start working on it. Most MSW programs are provided on a part time basis to accommodate working parents and professionals. While I myself initially wanted to obtain my Masters in Psychology, I realize how fortunate I was that I earned an MSW instead. The MSW degree is standardized throughout all Universities that offer the MSW. Because of that, licensing boards and insurance companies accept the MSW without requiring additional coursework.

Ask some of your friends who earned an MS or MA in Psychology how many more courses they had to take to become licensed. With an MSW, the LCSW is hopefully your next step in your professional development. The MSW is probably the most marketable degree in the human services and social services field. You can feel confident, and competent, that your MSW was a worthwhile academic endeavor and investment.

The socio-cultural and developmental history, a.k.a. the social history, is a primary staple required of the SSW. Writing a good social history depends on your education and training, but there are some common denominators found in professionally competent social history reports performed by a School Social Worker.

THE STRENGTH-BASED APPROACH TO SCHOOL SOCIAL WORK:

The School Social Worker (SSW) writes many, if not hundreds, of social histories every year. It seems that we tend to concentrate on the negative aspects of the student's life, more than the positive.

We believe that if we can identify the adversities that may be contributing to the "adverse impact" on a student's academic performance, we may have found the answer to their learning problem(s). It therefore seems natural to focus on a student's limitations and deficits when we are searching for explanations of under achievement, poor academic performance and behavioral or emotional problems. We are rarely, if ever, asked to look for reasons a student might be doing well in life and in school!

CAVEMAN WISDOM: "We know what we are but not what we may be."
By: Ophelia in Hamlet

In order for a social history to be comprehensive we should also explore the student's family's strengths and/or their protective factors; i.e. resiliency and talents. Resiliency can be defined as the ability to manifest the positive features of life, despite an abundance of adversity. Some children can spring back to life and successfully achieve great things after adversity, while others cannot. The child that can is said to manifest "resiliency"; surviving and thriving despite their significant troubles.

When gathering the background information for your social history, you are obviously looking for all aspects of the student's life that can help you and the SEC team understand why the student is struggling academically or emotionally. Good, we need to do that. But when writing our reports, it also helps the SEC team when a student's strengths are noted and discussed as well. It is, in a manner of speaking, an opportunity for the parents to speak about their child and family in a positive manner and balance the view of their child as a "whole" individual.

"Strength-based" reporting avoids pathological labels, while still acknowledging the student's struggles and specific needs. When the SEC team reviews the educational report from the teacher and the student observation report from another professional, both the positives and negatives, the student's strengths and weaknesses, are inherent aspects of those guided questionnaires and reports. As School Social Workers, we need to be more sensitive and aware of the student's strengths as well.

We can explore their many individual strengths and talents when describing: their personality traits; their hobbies and interests, what they do well; their socialization skills with peers; their family relationships; their talents-i.e. (music, art, athletics, reading, Legos construction (yes- Legos counts as a possible mechanical/spatial talent often seen in those who become engineers and architects!); cooking/culinary arts; auto mechanics; construction; Tech Ed.; electronics and computers, etc.). If you look for it, you will find that most students have some sort of **emerging** strength and talent. (i.e. Emerging means that children are not finished or complete individuals yet, so their talents do not have to be totally completed either).

Some school districts may even require that the School Social Worker interview the student as part of the social history. This way the SSW can discuss the student's likes and dislikes, dreams and aspirations, interests and talents first hand. Not a bad idea!

SSWs may also administer various standardized rating scales that provide "strength based" measures. The **Behavioral and Emotional Rating Scale (BERS-2)** is just one of many. It provides (5) strength-based subscales, e.g. interpersonal strength, family involvement, intrapersonal strength, school functioning, and affective strength. Another "strength based" rating scale is the **School Success Profile (SSP)** measuring the domains of one's neighborhood, school, friends, and family providing strength based variables for student wellbeing, behavior, and school performance.

There are many rating scales that can be utilized to pin point specific areas of strengths and weaknesses desired or needed to describe a student in a comprehensive manner. We are all more than what is in our educational record, more than a simple IQ score, more than what a teacher says we can or cannot do. We are not two dimensional, good-bad, or strong-weak, so we should not describe a student's life in our social history as if they were.

CAVEMAN WISDOM: "Youth would be an ideal state if it came a little later in life".
By: Herbert Henry Asquit.

CAVEMAN WISDOM: "If a man will begin with certainties, he shall end in doubts: but if he will be content to begin with doubts, he shall end in certainties".
By: Francis Bacon.

CAVEMAN WISDOM:-"Do what you can, with what you have, where you are".
By: Theodore Roosevel

THE COMMON DENOMINATORS: SCHOOL SOCIAL WORK DUTIES AND RESPONSIBILITIES:

CAVEMAN WISDOM: "One person can make a difference, and everyone should try".
By: John Fitzgerald Kennedy

There are several common denominators with regard to the duties and responsibilities of a School Social Worker as it relates to the day to day practice of School Social Work services; these include, but are not limited to:
- **ATTENDANCE;**
- **SOCIO-CULTURAL AND DEVELOPMENTAL HISTORY ASSESSMENT;**
- **STUDENT COUNSELING;**
- **COMMUNITY RESOURCES;**
- **HOMELESS RESOURCES;**
- **CRISIS INTERVENTION;**
- **RISK/THREAT ASSESSMENT; and**
- **SPECIAL EDUCATION.**

(A) ATTENDANCE: [Excessive absenteeism/truancy/excessive tardies/school refusal].

THE SCHOOL SOCIAL WORKER AND ATTENDANCE:

Schools receive federal and state funding based on student attendance. In many school systems, the School Social Worker (SSW) acts like a Truancy Officer. That means the SSW tracks students with poor attendance, and provides some level of intervention.

Acting as the School Social Worker for your school district "could" mean one of your responsibilities might be taking a student and his parent to Juvenile Court, for being in violation of the state's mandatory school attendance law, and/or providing case management counseling.

Motivating the student and family to get the student to attend school on a regular basis is both labor-intensive and very difficult to accomplish. There are many reasons that this is so hard to accomplish, and it has been my experience that an undiagnosed emotional problem (anxiety, depression, parental mental illness, etc) is a big part of that problem.

Effective SSW interventions might involve consulting with teachers and administrators regarding school system procedures and reviewing what the Guidance Counselor and Teacher policies are as well as the approved SSW interventions. (All vary district-by-district and state-by-state).

Students and their parents will react far more positively when the student's teacher calls the home telling the parent and student how concerned they are about the student's excessive absences, then when a School Social Worker calls. You get an entirely different reaction. Any guesses why?

It has been my experience that if attendance is big part of the School Social Workers duties, it can easily become about 60-75% of the SSW's day-day responsibilities.

Over the years I have come to the conclusion that attendance issues can be divided into eight sub-groups:

1) Parents with mental health issues/personality disorders
2) Students with mental health issues
3) Chronic Illness
4) Victimization by bullies
5) Academic inadequacies, i.e. undetected learning disabilities and slow learner profiles
6) Child abuse/neglect and families with severely unstable living situations
7) Long term divorce and custody conflicts
8) Intentional truancy/skipping school without parental knowledge/antisocial behavior (usually high school)

The first two attendance sub-groups are *PARENTS AND/OR STUDENTS WITH MENTAL HEALTH DISORDERS*:

This will be my mantra for all of the sub-groups: start off with a private SSW parent conference, then if necessary, a student support team meeting with the parent and teachers. Find out what is going on at home and at school. Find out about the student's, and the parent's, emotional sensitivities and health issues.

You need to be involved with the student and his family enough to know whether or not mental health problems are a valid concern. Observation of the student in school, parent interviews, as well as teacher and parent rating scales, can assist you in making an accurate determination. Knowing the family first hand is just good old fashioned case management and social work practice. Get to know the student and the family first hand, without judgment, and be sure it is conflict free, i.e. no threats of court action, etc. You should be their primary school support and resource professional representing the school district. You won't be able to accomplish this very effectively if your only goal is to take the parents to court under the mandatory school attendance law in your state.

NIMH Mental Illness Facts: Mental illnesses are medical conditions that disrupt a person's thinking, feeling, mood, ability to relate to others and daily functioning. Just as diabetes is a disorder of the pancreas, mental illnesses are medical/neurological conditions that often result in a diminished capacity for coping with the ordinary demands of life. They may also alter one's social, behavioral, and emotional reactions.

Serious mental illnesses include major depression, schizophrenia, bipolar disorder, obsessive-compulsive disorder (OCD), panic disorder, posttraumatic stress disorder (PTSD) and borderline personality disorder. The good news about mental illness is that management, and sometimes recovery, is possible.

Mental illnesses can affect persons of any age, race, religion, or income. Mental illnesses are not the result of personal weakness, lack of character, or poor upbringing. Mental illnesses are treatable. Most people diagnosed with a serious mental illness can experience relief from their symptoms by actively participating in an individual treatment plan provided by the appropriate licensed professional, i.e., psychiatrist, psychologist, medical doctor, social worker, etc.

In addition to pharmacological treatment, psychosocial treatments such as cognitive behavioral therapy, interpersonal therapy, peer support groups and other community services can also be effective components of a treatment plan and that assists with recovery.

School phobia, social anxiety, OCD, depression, and many other *mental health disorders can and do emerge, and are observable, in the Elementary School years*.
The old adage that children could not/would not develop these types of mental disorders is just that, an old and outdated adage.

Check out the National Institute of Mental Health (NIMH) website for child and adolescent psychiatric disorders. It will offer good research data on symptom pictures, prevalence, occurrence, age of onset, treatment, etc.

Adolescence is a developmental stage when serious mental health disorders show up. The biggies are: Bipolar Disorder, Schizophrenia, Major Depression, Substance Abuse, Anorexia, OCD, and fear of peer judgment (School phobia and Social Anxiety), to name a few.

In other words, mental health problems can occur at any age and in any grade.

NIMH: Important Fact about Mental Illness and Recovery.
(NIMH website)

- Mental illnesses are serious medical illnesses. They cannot be overcome through "will power" and are not related to a person's "character" or intelligence. Mental illness falls along a continuum of severity. Even though mental illness is widespread in the population, the main burden of illness is concentrated in a much smaller proportion-about 6 percent, or 1 in 17 Americans-who live with a serious mental illness. The National Institute of Mental Health reports that **One in four adults-approximately 57.7 million Americans-experience a mental health disorder in a given year**
- The U.S. Surgeon General reports that **10 percent of children and adolescents in the United States suffer from serious emotional and mental disorders** that cause significant functional impairment in their day-to-day lives at home, in school and with peers.
- The World Health Organization has reported that **four of the 10 leading causes of disability in the US and other developed countries are mental disorders. By 2020, Major Depressive illness will be the leading cause of disability in the world for women and children.**
- Mental illness usually strikes individuals in the prime of their lives, often during adolescence and young adulthood. All ages are susceptible, but the young and the old are especially vulnerable.
- Without treatment the consequences of mental illness for the individual and society are staggering: unnecessary disability, unemployment, substance abuse, **homelessness,** inappropriate incarceration, suicide and wasted lives; The economic cost of untreated mental illness is more than 100 billion dollars each year in the United States. The best treatments for serious mental illnesses today are highly effective; between 70 and 90 percent of individuals have significant reduction of symptoms and improved quality of life with a combination of pharmacological and psychosocial treatments and supports.
- With appropriate and effective medication, and a wide range of services tailored to their specific needs, most people who live with serious mental illnesses can significantly reduce the impact of their illness and find a satisfying measure of achievement and independence. A key concept is to develop expertise in developing strategies to manage the illness process.
- Early identification and treatment is of vital importance; By ensuring access to the treatment and recovery supports that are proven effective, recovery is accelerated and the further harm related to the course of illness is minimized.

Anxiety disorders are more common than you might think. You may start out with an infant and young child that is just temperamentally shy and sensitive. This can then progress into separation anxiety. Later on it often turns into social anxiety and then school phobia. If it continues unabated, it can turn into various Anxiety Disorders and/or Major Affective Disorders.

Although **school refusal** is not a clinical disorder according to the Diagnostic and Statistical Manual of Mental Disorders, Fifth Edition, it can be associated with several psychiatric disorders, including Separation Anxiety Disorder, Social Phobia, and Conduct Disorder. Therefore it is critical that students who are refusing to go to school receive a comprehensive evaluation by a mental health professional.

Common symptoms of school refusal behavior include anxiety, depression, withdrawal, fatigue, crying, and physical complaints such as stomachaches and headaches. More disruptive symptoms may include tantrums, noncompliance, arguing, refusal to move, running away from school and/or home, and aggression. Many children and adolescents with school refusal behavior show a wide range of constantly changing behaviors.

There is usually an obvious developmental spectrum at work here. Remain mindful of how the child's early neo-natal temperament and childhood temperament is the frame work and foundation for personality development, and the predisposition for later developing mental health disorders. No child grows up with the expectation at age 5 that "I'm not ever going to go to school and nobody can make me". Something happens that changes their outlook. It's our job to discover what happened to change their view of going to school.

Providing the parents with community resources, such as good mental health therapy centers and/or Pastoral Counseling, might be just what the doctor ordered. Most counseling in the school setting should be related to school issues anyway, and not about the onset of serious mental health disorders.

Helping students solve their week to week peer drama problems regarding their friendship, and how to improve test taking strategies, is referred to as "Counseling", i.e. problem solving. Guidance Counselors, SSWs, and SPs can help in these cases.

Helping a 15 year old cope with and understand the onset of their symptoms related to Major Depression with suicidal ideation; or Schizophrenia with bizarre thinking and delusions; or Bipolar Disorder, with severe hyperactivity and sleep deprivation and substance abuse; or daily Panic Attacks, is referred to as "Therapy".

The practice of psychotherapy is regulated by the state Board of Medicine that licenses Psychiatrists (M.D.); the Board of Psychology that licenses Clinical Psychologists (LCP); and the Board of Social Work that licenses Clinical Social Workers (LCSW). If you are not licensed by the state to practice psychotherapy, and you attempt to diagnose and treat somebody for a mental disorder, you are legally liable for a malpractice suit.

Knowing about your community resources is a primary School Social Worker responsibility. Helping families connect to various social support systems is common. There are families who are homeless, or on the verge of becoming homeless.

Many have no medical health insurance and need to apply for Medicaid, and find out where the Public Health clinic is. Housing and financial assistance are also common needs for many families that a School Social Worker works with. Many families need assistance with food. Many churches in most communities are excellent sources for assistance in such situations.

If there are significant medical or psychiatric issues adversely affecting the student in school, referral to the special education committee and/or the section 504 committees for a **screening** can provide much needed, and appropriate, class room interventions. I will not review, in great detail, the *IDEA Special Education Law and Section 504 of the ADA federal law)*. Every SSW needs to read and learn all about these federal school based laws and become intimately familiar with their provisions. *(look them up-IDEA and section 504 of ADA).*

The third attendance sub-group encompasses MEDICAL ILLNESS:

Start off with a private SSW parent conference and/or a student support team meeting with the parent. Find out what is going on. .

Anytime there is excessive absenteeism, reasons are usually muddled. Excused absences are usually only allowed if they are due to medical illness and hospitalization, with a Doctor's note or parent's note/ phone call describing the illness. Unexcused absences include: family vacations and all unverified and unreported absences. Even verified and approved absences due to medical illness can become excessive, and make it impossible for the student to keep up with the classwork in school. If a child's illness is prolonged, consider referring the student to the **Homebound Coordinator** for consideration of a Homebound Teacher. These Teachers teach the student in their home during their period of illness. The School Nurse and Guidance Counselor are also good resources in such cases.

Eligibility for Homebound Instruction will require medical documentation from the student's physician of a serious, but temporary, medical condition that requires that the student not attend school. The student's application will be reviewed by the appropriate administrative personnel for Homebound Instruction, and if found to be eligible, the student will be provided with a Teacher that comes to the student's home and teaches for several hours of the day, but usually never the usual 6-7 hours.

If the medical illness is related to a more serious condition and more permanent in nature, and the student can attend school, but may require classroom accommodations, refer the student to the SEC for a special education assessment and/or section 504 Committee for classroom accommodations.

The fourth attendance sub-group is VICTIMIZATION BY BULLYING:

CAVEMAN WISDOM: Start off with an SSW parent conference and/or a student support team meeting with the parents and teachers. Find out what is going on from the students perspective, the teachers perspective, and the parent's perspective. You may find out that the student has a history of lying, or manifests signs of an anxiety disorder, or is extremely shy and timid, and feels that if a student bumps in to them or messes with them in the halls, they considered it bullying. Maybe it is.

Many schools have **anti-bullying programs**. I have often noted that schools usually address these issues through their Guidance Counselors.

One or two classroom guidance lessons per year about bullying are just not enough! The entire school must take on an anti-bullying mentality. Teachers need to provide omnipresence in their classrooms, and especially the hallways between classes, and never tolerate bullying of any kind, i.e., teasing, harassment, or aggression, whether it is verbal, gestural or physical; and also be aware of obvious peer group exclusions of students that just don't seem to fit in.

Teachers and administrators need to be in front of their classrooms between class transitions and on the playground in order to observe student behaviors. It seems like bullying is done is a secretive and extremely quick and fast manner, and always when and where it seems that no one else sees it occur.

Many students report that most teachers and administrators are frequently dismissive, and don't take their reports seriously. This can leave lifelong scars in a bullied victims psyche. Even if the student feels he/she is bullied, but in reality maybe is not, and it is determined to be a case that the student is just being extremely shy and emotionally sensitive, giving that student 5 minutes to process their feelings with a teacher or administrator can make a huge difference in that student's life.

The fifth attendance sub-group regards ACADEMIC INADEQUACIES: UNDETECTED LEARNING DISABILITIES and SLOW LEARNER PROFILE.

CAVEMAN WISDOM: Start off with a private parent conference and/or a student support team meeting with the parents. Find out what is going on.

Academic inadequacies and specific learning disabilities occur in all age groups and socio-economic strata. There are many different types. Students, who feel they cannot keep up with their peers at the rate the curriculum is being taught, often develop school refusal behaviors. They complain of stomachaches and headaches and other various somatic symptoms to get out of going to school.

Why do they feel inadequate? Many students manifest undiagnosed learning disabilities, and sub-clinical depression and anxiety disorders. Obsessive-compulsive personality types who are perfectionists, find out they are not perfect, straight "A" students.

Maybe a favorite grandparent or relative just died and the student is experiencing a severe grief reaction that has resulted in a temporary loss of interest in school.

Feeling inadequate is a complex cognitive thought. The human mind has created complex computers and sent men to the moon, yet we find it hard to understand how the mind works, and when it falters, we are even more perplexed. Unraveling feelings of academic inadequacy takes a great deal of investigation into one's life. Dig deep, and keep digging.

Most schools have "Student Support Teams" that meet informally to discuss students who are struggling academically. The team develops academic and social strategies to assist the student. The School Social Worker and/or School Psychologist are often times part of these teams and can offer relevant social and psychological support ideas.

The sixth attendance sub-group regards CHILD ABUSE AND NEGLECT

CAVEMAN WISDOM: Start off with a parent conference and/or a student support team meeting with the parent. Find out what is going on.

Child abuse and neglect often creates within a child a sense of self-doubt and low self-worth. Children become depressed and/or anxious and develop active somatic symptoms that result in school refusal and school anxiety behaviors.

Talking with a parent about what is going on can and should be confidential between just you and the parent, UNLESS, you suspect child abuse and/or neglect. Then, you have a legal obligation to report your suspicions to the Department of Social Services.

CAVEMAN WISDOM: If a teacher or school administrator tells you THEY suspect abuse or neglect, and they want YOU to make the call, DON'T DO IT! That is second hand information and social services needs to hear it from the source. But be ready to hear all sorts of school policies that differ with the "real law".

Any suspicions "an educational professional" has about abuse or neglect, has the same legal obligation to report to Social Services that you do as a School Social Worker.

Only the **primary informant should report what they suspect and why, otherwise the information is second hand information**, and believe me, it gets really muddled when you don't know anything else but what someone else tells you. It can become a SSW nightmare.

Is the student home alone all day while the parent is at work? Does that constitute child neglect; if the child is not sick, but is home with a parent, and there is no other reported reason for the child to miss school, does that constitute neglect? Does the parent stay home with the child but make excuses for the student; is there a Munchausen syndrome present?

Does the child manifest an undiagnosed social anxiety disorder, and over the years has become a school phobic, appearing to be oppositional and defiant, and just wore out their parent's energy and efforts to get them to school? Is this a neglectful parent? Or a family in need of your support and possibly a referral to a mental health counselor?

CAVEMAN WISDOM: "I have yet to see any problem, however complicated, which, when you looked at it in the right way, did not become still more complicated". By: Paul Anderson.

The seventh attendance sub-group is LONG TERM DIVORCE AND CUSTODY ISSUES:

When there is a contentious and acrimonious divorce and custody situation, it complicates everything in the child's world. Some children are more resilient than others, but most are affected to some extent no matter what.

I am sure many of you are from divorced homes and know exactly what I am talking about. The more acrimonious and hostile the parents are towards each other, the more the children suffer.

Marion Gindes, Ph.D writes in her article "The Psychological Effects of Relocation for Children of Divorce" in the Journal of the American Academy of Matrimonial Lawyer:

"The divorce of parents significantly undermines their children's sense of security and stability. The two people upon whom the child is dependent are no longer equally accessible to the child and the foundation of the child's world is splintered".

"From the child's perspective, the best of all possible worlds, after parental divorce, includes parents who are amicable, do not display overt hostility, can communicate with each other about the child, and live close enough to each other so that child can have the same playmates when with either parent. These conditions maximize the potential for the child developing strong, positive relationships with both parents as well as for both parents' involvement in the child's school and extracurricular activities and for frequent and regular contact with the non-residential parent".

"When a residential or custodial parent, then, seeks to move to a different geographic region, the best possible post-divorce scenario for children is threatened. The wish to relocate poses the most dramatic example of the conflicting needs and wishes of parents and children and of the conflicting needs and wishes of custodial and noncustodial parents.

For the most part, children do not wish to leave the environment in which they live nor do they wish to leave their noncustodial parent, who also does not want them to go. Parent and child relocation, which has become a major problem facing mental health and legal professionals, is, however, inevitable in a mobile society".

"Constance Ahrons uses the term "binuclear" to describe the post-divorce family. According to her, the binuclear family consists of two households, with the child living in both. The binuclear family includes stepparents, stepsiblings, even former spouses of stepparents as well as parents, full siblings and half-siblings. While this is a broad definition of the post-divorce family constellation, it highlights the interconnectedness of the various people involved".

One child on my caseload missed over 15 days because of court hearings requiring that the child be present. They were counted as unexcused by the school. The mother was the custodial parent and lived in one state. The father lived in another state and was the non-custodial parent with joint custody. He filed four petitions in one year in his state to try and change the custody ruling and child-support payments. The mother and the student had to take time off from work and school to make the two-day drive to the father's state to attend various court hearings. It added up to 15 days in one year. The Assistant Principal wanted me to file an "educational neglect" petition against the parent because she **did not believe** the mother was telling her the truth despite paper work that documented the mother's story.

What can you do? What can you say? Life can be difficult, and even more difficult to understand people's motives at times. Was this mother being neglectful? Would an attendance petition have helped? Would the JD court even accept my petition based on those facts?

Many Guidance Counselors and SSWs run divorce adjustment groups at school for students experiencing divorce adjustment problems. This can be an excellent resource for parents and students and can definitely help a child cope with the many variables they must face. This adjustment can take months, years, or a lifetime.

The eighth attendance sub-group is INTENTIONAL TRUANCY/JUVENILE DELINQUENCY

What is the definition of truancy? ***Truancy is a legal term, and may have different definitions in different states and cities- (look it up).***

Generally this is when a student skips school / cuts classes and the parent is unaware of the absence. If the child is at home and the parent knows it, it is not truancy, it is an "unexcused absence", and it should not technically be referred to as truancy.

It is my opinion that there are very few real " truants" in the elementary school grades. The percentage is low even in middle school but can grow and become problematic in high school. The reason students become truants, is related to the issues discussed in the previous six sub-groups. In high school, you should also consider substance-abuse factors and juvenile delinquency and/or antisocial behavior.

Leo Tolstoy's famous quote is very informative and a family therapists mantra: **"Happy families are all alike; every unhappy family is unhappy in its own way"**.

Maybe you could say this about truants: **"All happy students attend school regularly and are mostly alike; but unhappy students that skip school, skip for their own reasons"**.

Sometimes a child's absence is just a "mental health day"; who hasn't taken one of those. In fact, who doesn't need to take one? We all need an R&R day at some time, and so do kids. Their job (school) is very stressful. The problem is, when a student takes an R&R day, it is usually without parental permission, and there is no adult supervision. This can often mean TROUBLE in many cases. Pregnancy, substance abuse, juvenile delinquent activities, etc. are common problems associated with chronic truancy. The lack of an adequate education and not graduating from high school can then become a distinct possibility.

Sometimes the "good truant", just wants to stay home and rest. He/she isn't going outside and there is no trouble making lurking in the air. Maybe his/her parents even allow this two or three times a year. Is that ever ok? Is that considered educational neglect?

In most situations, when you dig deep enough, you will find that it is because of abuse, neglect, academic inadequacy, depression, anxiety, substance abuse, sleep deprivation, or juvenile delinquency. Our job is to figure out what is causing the absences, and problem solve with the family to minimize, or completely stop, all school absences. Good Luck!!

In high school a student may feel that school just doesn't offer them anything worthwhile. Maybe the student wants to be an electrician or hair stylist, and there are no vocational programs; and algebra, geometry, calculus, biology, English, and world history just doesn't make their school days very enjoyable. They just don't see the value in these subject areas when all they want to do is fix broken down automobiles or air conditioners. They are not motivated. Nothing they are being taught has a real world connection.

But, these students are bucking the politically correct DOE and local school board mantra; our society doesn't need more Tec-Ed programs! Students don't need music and PE anymore! America needs STEM programs! All students need algebra! All students need a second language! When school boards say this, are they neglecting a select group of students? Maybe, maybe not. It is a complicated question.

Forget all the lectures about the value of a high school education; instead help them find something of value that they can identify with and find useful with regard to their future plans. Help the family check out GED and Voc-Tech programs. And for older students, say 17-18 and older, adult education programs are an option. There are certification programs for all sorts of vocational careers, but you have to know where to look.

Problem solving doesn't necessarily mean cramming someone else's values about education down their throats; it means solving the problem in a way that it still has social redeeming value, but also is meaningful and useful to **THEM:** more than to **YOU**!

CAVEMAN WISDOM: "Your time is limited, so don't waste it living someone else's life. Don't let the noise of others' opinions drown out your own inner voice. And most important, have the courage to follow your heart and intuition." By: Steve Jobs

CAVEMAN WISDOM: Education is what remains after one has forgotten what one has learned in school. By: Albert Einstein

Remember your developmental neuroscience; their Pre-Frontal Cortex is not fully developed until around age 25; so, their judgment, good decision making skills, and long term planning skills are still immature even in high school!

Is homeschooling an answer? Parents can legally opt to "homeschool" their child as well. That is different than "homebound" schooling. **Homeschooling** is where **the parent is the teacher**. Different states and city school boards will have different qualifications for homeschooling, so get to know the regulations in your area.

It is usually not thought to be a very good idea, as many parents are just not qualified academically or personally, to teach their child adequately and competently.

CAVEMAN WISDOM: If a parent ever wants to re-enroll their child back into public school later on after having been HOME SCHOOLED, but they **never kept track of grades or test results**, **or listed the academic subjects** taught; and, **never had their child take national standardized tests**, they may not be admitted into the grade they think they should be in. Some schools, maybe most schools, may not enroll that student at the grade level that the parent and student desire, citing a lack of documented curriculum and testing results that point to a student's academic preparedness. It can be a nightmare for the unprepared family who has opted to HOME SCHOOL.

Home schooling really does not work out well when a parent opts to home school just because they are tired fighting with their child who is not attending school. They are tired of the School Social Worker calling them, or the school's administrators calling for the umpteenth time to schedule a Student Support Team Meeting.

The bottom line is, of course, that the parent is unable, or unwilling, to get their child to attend school! SSWs can be very supportive to parents if we look at their side of the problem, and not blame them for the problem. It is not always their fault. (It wasn't their fault that their child had schizophrenia or autism, despite earlier research that said it was. It may not be their fault that their child developed school phobia). But it could be! So you have to be a really good "clinician" to figure it out; to figure out the parent's motivation and psychological make-up and the student's motivation and psychological make-up.

It is my opinion that many parents typically get a bad rap from school administrators. Everyone finds it way too easy to blame the parents. Life is much more complicated than that. I have worked with dedicated and loving parents who have children that are diagnosed with depression, early onset bipolar disorder, and anxiety disorders and despite tremendous effort and motivation to get their child to school, cannot get their child to attend school regularly. We need to walk a mile in their shoes before we put all the blame on them.

On the other hand, some parents are quite competent at homeschooling and do a wonderful job. They may utilize commercial curriculums purchased off the Internet or purchase the same schoolbooks that are utilized in their school district, keeping meticulous track of subjects, tests and grades, etc. Home schooling parents can also join home-school parent groups and trade off teaching different subjects. This variation offers the child a controlled small "class" environment and controlled socialization experiences.

The National Center for Educational Statistics cites that parents give many different reasons for homeschooling their children. In 2007 the most common reason parents gave was a desire to provide religious or moral instruction (36 percent of students). This reason was followed by a concern about the school environment (such as safety, drugs, or negative peer pressure) (21 percent); dissatisfaction with academic instruction (17 percent); and "other reasons" including family time, finances, travel, and travel distance (14 percent).

Parents for about 7 percent of home schooled students cited the desire to provide their child with a non-traditional approach to education as the most important reason for home schooling, and the parents of another 6 percent of students cited a child's health problems or special needs.

More than 2 million U.S. students in grades K-12 were home-schooled in 2010, accounting for nearly four percent of all school-aged children, according to the National Home Education Research Institute.

Believe it or not; studies suggest that those who go on to college will outperform their peers. Students coming from a home schooling background graduated college at a higher rate than their peers -- 66.7 percent compared to 57.5 percent -- and earned higher grade point averages along the way.

Regional homeschooling associations are getting better and better at organizing their academic activities, and ***research shows competently homeschooled children do just fine on most standardized achievement tests, and attend the college of their choice with excellent long term success. (look it up),***

CAVEMAN WISDOM: Truancy cases are labor intensive. Not all school divisions require their School Social Workers to deal with attendance and truancy issues. Some cities have Truant Officers that are employed by the Juvenile Court system separate from the School Board. Some school districts however, ask their SSW to be "truant officers" as well as "School Social Workers". Doing both the SSW special education component and attendance component can become overwhelming.

(B) SOCIO-CULTURAL AND DEVELOPMENTAL HISTORY ASSESSMENT: Social histories performed for special education evaluations.

The School Social Worker and the SOCIO-CULTURAL HISTORY ASSESSMENT:

The IDEA (*Individuals with Disabilities Education Act)-(look it up)* is a federal law regarding the provision of special education services. It requires that every school system that receives federal funding abide by the IDEA provisions and requirements.

"Child Find" is one of those provisions, requiring schools to **"screen"**, (not necessarily evaluate), any child **"suspected"** of exhibiting a significant disability that might be having an adverse impact on a their academic progress and/or participation in the educational program.

CAVEMAN WISDOM: While learning disabilities and some emotional disorders have an adverse impact on academic performance; what about the emotional disorders that result **in a lack of participation in the educational program**. i.e. bipolar disorder, major depression, ADHD, etc. that result in frequent school absences, behavior problems and suspensions? Are they not just as relevant and also eligible for special education services, **even if their grades are still acceptable?** These are not true conduct problems when a mental disorder is the root cause. That is why they are referred to by mental health professionals as "Neuro-behavioral" disorders.

IDEA also requires that a multi-disciplinary team of professionals, including the School Social Worker, provide this screening.

If the SPED team feels that there is a clear suspicion that a disability might be causing an adverse impact on academic performance, or a lack of participation in the educational program, then they must recommend a comprehensive assessment to rule out the possibility that one of the 14 types of educational disabilities does exist.

Those 14 educational disabilities listed in IDEA are:
autism, deafness, deaf-blindness, developmental delay, emotional disability, hearing impairment/deafness, intellectual disability, multiple disabilities, orthopedic disability, other health impairment (usually ADHD), specific learning disability, speech or language impairments, traumatic brain injury, and visual impairments/blindness.

The SSW usually assists in the comprehensive assessment by performing a socio-cultural and developmental history, in order to rule out evidence of *exclusionary factors, i.e. cultural, environmental, or economic disadvantages. (look it up).*

If there is significant evidence that one of these **exclusionary factors** is primarily contributing to a student's poor academic performance, the student may not be found to be eligible for special education services, if there are no other contributing factors.

So you can see, the Socio-cultural and developmental history (social history) can be a very important piece of the comprehensive assessment puzzle. When it is done right it contributes significantly to the process of eligibility determination, as required in the IDEA provisions.

The six components of a comprehensive special education assessment in accordance with IDEA are:

1-**Educationa**l-conducted by the student's teacher, describing grades, academic and behavioral strengths and weaknesses, standardized testing results.

2-**Medical**-conducted by the student's physician or a contracted school physician to rule out the existence of any significant medical issues.

3-**Psychologica**l-the School Psychologist will perform a psychological assessment that usually includes a cognitive assessment (IQ), full range of academic achievement, and a full range of rating scales that measure social, behavioral, and emotional issues.

4- **Socio-Cultural (Social History)** -the School Social Worker conducts a parent interview (usually in their primary residence) to collect relevant information regarding: family composition and dynamics; pregnancy, birth, neo-natal temperament, early childhood development, educational history, medical history, and strengths and weaknesses regarding social and emotional functioning. (See below for detailed components).

5-**Vision**-assess visual acuity and any related visual disorders.

6-**Hearing**-assess hearing acuity and any related hearing impairment.

The focus of the comprehensive assessment for the School Social Worker is the **Socio-Cultural and developmental history.**

This assessment includes a parent interview by the SSW that reviews a student's life history, and includes the following areas of inquiry: pregnancy, birth and delivery, neonatal temperament, family composition and dynamics, residential stability, environmental habitability and suitability, educational history and stability (school attendance, geographical relocations, peer relationships), mental health history (parent and student), medical history (parent and student), as well as social and emotional functioning in the home, neighborhood, and school environments.

It is a good idea for the SSW to utilize an approved "guided-interview questionnaire" that covers the vast array of important socio-cultural and life domain questions. You must be knowledgeable about child development, medical disorders, psychiatric disorders, pediatric health, genetic disorders, family dynamics, and abnormal child development.

(C): STUDENT COUNSELING: Counseling students at school regarding social, emotional, behavioral and/or academic problems.

The School Social Worker and COUNSELING:

SSWs are frequently asked to provide counseling in the school to students regarding a wide range of problems. The Guidance Counselors and School Psychologists are also good counseling resources, but the SSW may be the only one they ask to intervene when a **home visit** is required in order to talk to the student's parents about a child's emotional or behavioral problems. Home visits are for the most part, the meat and potatoes of the SSW domain.

Teachers and other school personnel will often ask the SSW to perform a home visit when there is chronic and excessive school absences; suspicion of school refusal behaviors; and when a parent conference has been requested and the parent either cannot, or will not, respond to school personnel efforts to meet at the school.

SSWs are not Child Abuse investigators, so if a teacher or school administrator wants you to make a home visit because they suspect child abuse or neglect, don't do it; that is not our responsibility, and **we are not legally or ethically authorized (or trained) to investigate** child abuse and neglect.

The Department of Social Services/Child Protective Services in your City is the only legally authorized agency permitted to investigate child abuse and neglect. While we have a professional obligation to "**report any suspicions of child abuse and neglect**" **we do not have any obligation to <u>investigate</u> child abuse or neglect.**

Teachers and school personnel also have the same obligation to report suspicions of child abuse and neglect, so do not allow them to ask you to report their suspicions for them, that is their sole legal and ethically responsibility.

When a student may benefit from some form of individual counseling, Guidance Counselors, School Social Workers, School Psychologists, school mentoring programs, tutors, Big Brother and Big Sister programs, can also provide additional support and assistance, albeit more limited.

Mental health counseling, in my opinion, is not always effective when performed in the school setting. It has something to do with the *"therapeutic milieu"*, **and** *"therapeutic relationship"* **(look it up)**, and the development of trust and confidentiality.

The "therapeutic milieu" is an important factor in developing the "therapeutic relationship", which is based on trust and confidentiality. I have my doubts that that level of trust and privacy/confidentiality can happen in the school setting.

The parent is also not present during the counseling/therapy session, and frequently, even when performing individual therapy with children, their presence and "joining in" at the end of a session can be very supportive and beneficial to the child, (most of the time, not all the time).

Here is a good definition for "therapeutic milieu". Although usually used to denote the inpatient psychiatric hospital environment, those professionals that have engaged in private practice or mental health counseling at community Mental Health Centers, can identify with this definition.

- First, **milieu** is French for 'middle place' so you might think of it as a nice **"safe place"**.
- Milieu refers to the **people & all other social and physical factors in the environment with which the patient interacts**.
- This environment is designed **to provide a secure retreat** for person's whose capacities for coping with reality have deteriorated (people who just can't cope anymore).
- It offers opportunities to acquire adaptive coping skills (teaches you more effective ways or new ways to deal with problems) & lets the patient test these new coping skills in a secure, comfortable place.
- **Milieu protects & shelters the patient from perceived pain and terrifying stressors**. (the school setting can be perceived by some students as not being very safe or free from psychosocial stressors).
- This therapy supports the patient physiologically, provides pleasant and attractive sensory stimulation, and teaches patients & family members adaptive coping strategies.
- All personnel in the environment must work together to provide a caring, healing environment.

I wish I could define the school environment as a "safe place; free of pain and stressors", but it is not that kind of place for many students. It is sometimes "the identified stressor" in the life of those students with Autism Spectrum Disorders manifesting social skills deficits; students with school phobia/anxiety; students who are severely shy, timid, and fearful; and especially those students who are not eligible for IDEA or 504 services but are manifesting grossly inadequate academic performance (e.g. those students with a slow learner profile or with "borderline intellectual" deficits).

There are many other students who for one reason or another, simply just do not like school. While we should try to help these students cope and adjust, it may not be possible to accomplish this in the school environment that produces the same anxiety we are trying to help the student overcome. Some might say, but this is good, it is like "implosive therapy", the kind we use with phobics; good luck making that work when you only spend 20 minutes once a week or every two weeks with the student in a not so private conference room next to the Principal's office!

I wish it weren't so, because I love helping kids solve their own problems. There is no better feeling for a SSW, but I have rarely seen good privacy, strict confidentiality, and stable therapeutic relationships develop when working from the **educational/school** "*milieu*".

CAVEMAN WISDOM: It is extremely hard to attain therapeutic trust in a school environment. Individual counseling sessions compete with academic class time, maybe 10-15-20 minutes at best, mostly during their lunch break, (who doesn't need lunch)? or some other class time that is not academic, but that they hate to miss (art, music, PE); and it is usually in the school conference room with either the School Social Worker or School Psychologist, which everyone in the school knows only sees troubled kids; and which, just happens to be next to the Assistant Principal's office or the Guidance Counselor's office, or even worse, the Principal's office, where everyone knows only the trouble makers go. Where is the privacy and confidentiality? Where is the therapeutic milieu?

Remember the difference between School Social Work counseling and individual therapy. We can counsel students regarding school related issues; attendance, homework, peer relationship problems, etc. But psychotherapy / therapy for a mental disorder is another thing. It is my opinion that only licensed mental health professionals should be diagnosing mental disorders and/or providing individual psychotherapy and mental health therapy. The ethical policies concerning the respective state licensing boards of clinical social work and clinical psychology also think that way! Most school boards also have strict policies against SSWs and SPs performing **"psychotherapy"** with students.

In the context of mental health, **"counseling"** is generally used to denote a relatively brief treatment that is focused most upon solving asocial or behavior problems. It often targets a particular problematic situation and offers suggestions and advice for dealing with it.

"Therapy" and/or "Psychotherapy" on the other hand, is generally a long-term treatment process that focuses more on gaining insight into chronic psychological and emotional problems. The focus is on the patient's cognitive thought processes and their perceptions of being in the world rather than specific school problems.

In actual practice, there may be quite a bit of overlap between the two. A therapist may provide counseling with specific situations and a counselor may function in a psychotherapeutic manner.

Generally speaking, however, psychotherapy requires more skill than simple counseling. It is conducted by professionals trained and licensed by the state's respective licensing boards to practice psychotherapy; e.g., a psychiatrist, a licensed professional counselor, a licensed clinical social worker or licensed clinical psychologist. While a psychotherapist is qualified to provide counseling, a counselor may not possess the necessary training and skills (and legal authority) to provide psychotherapy.

There are times when a 504 plan or IEP may require either the School Psychologists (SP) or SSW to provide "social skills training" and/or "counseling" to an ADHD/ASD student, etc. If so, you are stuck, the 504 plan and IEP are legal documents, and you are bound to comply with the plan.

The full weight and authority of the federal government in the case of an IEP, and if it is a 504 plan, the Office of Civil Rights, ensures that a disabled student gets the help they deserve. (Just remember the difference between counseling and therapy).

You should try to be a part of the IEP or 504-plan team that is recommending counseling accommodations. If you feel they may have asked you to do something that is beyond your training and qualifications, you need to tell them why, and get the IEP/504 modified, with parental permission of course.

Counseling a student can be very rewarding. Just make sure you are counseling a student for the right reason, with the right counseling technique, and "do no harm".

Social support counseling, school social work counseling, and social skills training are not necessarily considered to be a "psychotherapeutic technique" (depending on someone's definition of course), and can be accomplished by the SSW in the school environment. Using the politically correct term, "school social work counseling" on the 504 and IEP plans may be more acceptable from an ethical and legal standpoint.

Providing "psychological counseling", "psychotherapy", or "therapy" is not so ethically or legally defensible, so beware of these terms if they are put into the IEP/504 and avoid providing "psychological counseling", "psychotherapy", or "therapy" whenever possible; unless you are authorized by the state, and the school board, and you have the training and education and are appropriately licensed to provide mental health services. Make sure you have the appropriate malpractice insurance as well! Getting your own from a private professional social work malpractice company is not a bad idea. Check out NASW for these resources.

CAVEMAN WISDOM: "I've learned that people will forget what you said, people will forget what you did, but people will never forget how you made them feel". By: Maya Angelou

CAVEMAN WISDOM: "When people show you who they are, believe them". By: Maya Angelou

(D): COMMUNITY RESOURCES: Referring parents to relevant community resources.

The School Worker and COMMUNITY RESOURCES:

The SSW is the one school professional that should know better than anyone else what the available community resources are, and how to help families connect to them. We need to find out what exists in our community and continue to network at every opportunity.

Many SSWs have excellent networking skills. Some have been able to officially get major businesses such as your local Walgreens, Wal Mart, Food Lion, etc. to provide book bags, school supplies, hygiene products, lice kits, etc., to the School Social Work Department. The SSW can then provide them to needy families on an as needed basis.

Businesses make excellent community resources. Many see it as their community duty and participate as a service obligation. Others might see it as good marketing. Whatever the reason, they make good friends to SSW departments.

SSWs are frequently asked to help families who experience temporary homelessness, and/or chronic homelessness. SSWs don't have to solve their homelessness, but we do need to know who can help them at The Department of Social Services and/or local churches, and what their phone numbers and points of contact are.

CAVEMAN WISDOM: Many times families experience significant, even severe, socio-economic adversity. Trying to do everything for everybody can often burn out a SSW in no time.

It is not our job as SSWs to solve all of our clients' problems, but we need to know who else can help and who to refer them to. We are **School Social Workers, with an emphasis on School**. Keep a detailed directory with names and phone numbers of the various community resources and agencies that can meet the needs of our many deserving students and their families. Do what you can and know the parameters of your SSW job duties and responsibilities, and develop a comprehensive community resources notebook and update it monthly. Network with your fellow SSWs for ideas and additional resources.

CAVEMAN WISDOM: "No one is useless in this world who lightens the burden of it to anyone else". By: Dickens

CAVEMAN WISDOM: "Poverty is like punishment for a crime you didn't commit." By Eli Khamarov

(E) HOMELESS RESOURCES: Providing needed resources for students and families that are homeless under the *(McKinney-Vento Act (look it up)*.

The School Social Worker and HOMELESSNESS RESOURCES:

The SSW will invariably encounter families that have become homeless for one reason or another. ***The McKinney-Vento Homeless Education Assistance Act*** is a federal law that ensures immediate enrollment and educational stability for homeless children and youth. McKinney-Vento provides federal funding to states for the purpose of supporting district programs that serve homeless students.

The SSW traditionally works to support families experiencing socio-economic hardship. Homeless families meet every definition. These families require labor-intensive assistance in order to provide a stable living environment for their children. The McKinney Vento Act helps School Social Work departments make this happen by focusing on a student's school stability.

Defining Homeless:

The McKinney-Vento Act defines homeless children as "individuals who lack a fixed, regular, and adequate nighttime residence." The act provides examples of children who would fall under this definition:

- Children and youth sharing housing due to loss of housing, economic hardship or a similar reason
- Children and youth living in motels, hotels, trailer parks, or camp grounds due to lack of alternative accommodations
- Children and youth living in emergency or transitional shelters
- Children and youth abandoned in hospitals
- Children and youth awaiting foster care placement
- Children and youth whose primary nighttime residence is not ordinarily used as a regular sleeping accommodation (e.g. park benches, etc.)
- Children and youth living in cars, parks, public spaces, abandoned buildings, substandard housing, bus or train stations
- Migratory children and youth living in any of the above situations

School District Responsibilities:

Local school districts must designate a homeless liaison to ensure that homeless children and youth are identified and served. The liaison must provide public notice to homeless families (in the community and at school), and facilitate access to school services including transportation. School districts are also required to track their homeless students and report that data annually to OSPI.The SSW has a legitimate role in assisting homeless families and it can be very rewarding when a good plan comes together. It can also be very labor intensive, as these families experience a wide range of socio-economic adversity and may require many community resources to become stable.

(F) CRISIS INTERVENTION: Debriefing students after the recent death of a student/teacher at their school, or significant school crises.

The School Social Worker and CRISES INTERVENTION:

Different school districts will most likely have their own unique crises intervention policy and guidelines. Response techniques and interventions should be well organized and thought out and compiled in a Crisis Management Handbook for all Schools and Departments to have at the ready. Training and crisis team intervention exercises also help with the smooth deployment in the future event there is a substantial crisis.

It is customary for the SSW to be involved at some degree and at some level. Many types of traumatic events can affect families and the student's ability to focus on school, or even attend school. Hurricanes, tornados, floods, and fires are some of the community wide events most often encountered.

Deaths of family members, and even pets, can cause some degree of hopefully, temporary disconnect with school. The suicide of a Teacher, student, or schoolmate is another type of traumatic event commonly encountered that often results in a rather profound impact on students, and Teachers, alike.

Providing "crises debriefing counseling" usually includes the School Social Worker (SSW), the School Psychologist (SP), and the Guidance Counselor (GC). Their roles are very similar: to assist those students, parents, and Teachers that are experiencing profound emotional distress to have an immediate opportunity to facilitate their feelings and emotions in a caring and supportive environment.

Offering follow up assistance for several weeks is also a good plan. Delayed trauma reactions are quite common. Providing families and students who continue to manifest rather significant symptoms with community resources, as well as Teachers with EAP counselor referrals, is common.

Sometimes the RED CROSS and FEMA may be involved, in cases of community wide events. Knowing all about your community resources is the SSW's best strength. Sometimes the SSW may require assistance as well, (care givers are prone to burnout and PTSD as well), so know yourself, and know who can help you when you may need supportive assistance.

It has ben my experience when there is an organized CRISIS TEAM and it has been deployed to cover a death of a student or Teacher under normal circumstances, there are usually too many people. The best *CRISIS TEAM"* is the local Guidance Counselor, SSW and SP assigned to the designated school. The students already know the GC, SSW and SP so they are familiar faces in a time of need.

Having a large group of strangers hanging around disrupting the school's routine only creates more anxiety in my opinion.

If after the local team has been deployed and find that the crisis requires more personnel, a "**STAND BY TEAM**" should then be deployed.

If it is a **major crisi**s such as a tornado, flood, fire, etc. with extensive community damage and trauma, the school CRISIS TEAM should have a well formulated plan authorized by the School Board and City that would stipulate when they should merge with FEMA and the RED CROSS. Remember, the local GC, SSW, and SP are usually victims of the same crisis is such a circumstance and will require needed assistance as well.

(G) RISK/THREAT ASSESSMENT:

The School Social Worker and RISK/ THREAT ASSESSMENT:

This chapter could be 200 pages long in and of itself. Please read as much as you can about this topic and become familiar with the research. Find a good workshop or two to go to. While SSWs will not be required to participate in a risk assessment frequently, when you are asked, you should know what to do, do it spontaneously, and do it competently.

The **National School Safety Center,** www.nsscl.org , **the Center for Disease Control and Prevention** (CDC) www.cdc.gov/youthviolence, and the Office of Juvenile Justice and Delinquency Prevention (OJJDP) have many resources appropriate to the SSW for review.

One private company that I personally like is **"Specialized Training Services"** out of San Diego. They offer nation wide training/workshops and have published many books relevant to **school violence, risk assessment, and crisis intervention**. **Reid Meloy, Ph.D., Kris Mohandie, Ph.D. and Anna Salter, Ph.D.** are three of the 17 experts in this company who I have high regard for and whose workshops I have attended and whose books I have personally read. I am sure there are many other companies and professionals who currently specialize in school violence and risk assessment. **(look it up)**. Since the Columbine tragedy, a new field of forensic social work and psychology has blossomed. Even the **Secret Service** has published risk assessment criteria for potential school related violence.

Just like crises intervention, risk assessment in the school usually involves the SSW to some degree at some level. Since the Columbine, Co tragedy and those school tragedies that have followed, most school districts have become very sensitive to threat issues in their school environment. Most schools have an entire Department dedicated to safe school practices, or at least a Coordinator for Safe Schools and Risk Management, that formally spells out a safe school initiative that includes a formal action plan for threat assessment.

The plan I am most familiar with involved: the student, teacher, Guidance Counselor, the SSW, the School Psychologist; and a School Administrator, usually designated as the School Safety Officer.

The Teacher and their Guidance Counselor are the first professionals to have contact with the student and initiate the assessment process. Teachers and Guidance Counselors usually know their student population better than anyone else. They will usually get a referral from a school administrator about a student who they feel may pose a risk because they have just made some type of threat at school either toward a specific individual or a general/vague threat. In either case, it is worth keeping track of such threats.

Threats are varied. The most common type of risk situation involves students that bring a weapon of some type to school, or threaten other students or Teachers with serious harm.

In many cases the student who has threatened to kill another student, or Teacher, has no real intention of killing the student or Teacher, (unless there is a weapon involved**), but you cannot take that chance and simply discipline the student.** To do nothing, and to not assess the student's risk for future violence, could leave the school liable for a lawsuit. No one has a crystal ball, no matter how well you think you know a student, it is better to evaluate the level of threat and make a multi-disciplinary decision.

Since the Guidance Counselor is the first person who may be able to identify the student immediately and assess the severity of the threat the student poses, the intervention might be over at that level; i.e. the Guidance Counselor and the Assistant Principal may be able to handle it with the student's parents, if the student and parents are well known and there are no questions about the severity or level of the threat, i.e., No opportunity, no specific names, no specific motive, no history of violence or weapons possession.

In other situations where the Guidance Counselor does not know the student very well, and the level of threat is unknown, a more comprehensive threat assessment is indicated.

A comprehensive multi-disciplinary threat assessment should involve the SSW, the School Psychologist, the Guidance Counselor, School Administrators, and the student's parents. The student is usually suspended pending the results of a formal multi-disciplinary threat assessment. The suspension is usually based on various disciplinary code infractions.

School Administrators, the Guidance Counselor, and the student's Teachers may be the only source for past history of threat behavior. Your first task is to document past behavior. What is that famous saying in psychology: **"the best predictor of future behavior is past behavior"**. Not always true, but a good indicator that something is going on in most cases.

The School Psychologist may perform a psychological evaluation with a focus on the student's behavior and any emotional issues. The Psychologist should provide both positive and negative descriptors of the student. Risky behavior and emotional instability is just as important as describing positive behavior and emotional stability. You need a comprehensive picture of the child that provides both strengths and weaknesses in order to assign a realistic level of threat.

The School Social Worker may be asked to do a social history with a focus on family dysfunction, a history of student suicide threats, and/or homicidal threats, conduct disorder, poor socialization skills, emotional instability, and/or a history of causing harm to animals. Most of these questions can only be answered by the student's parents.

The SSW should also investigate **protective factors**; describe the positive side of the student's family life and socio-economic stability; describe nurturing and supportive family relationships and the quality of the home environment.

Describe the student's positive social relationships with family members, siblings, and neighborhood peers; describe the lack of mental illness in family members; describe the student's positive hobbies and activities of daily living.

Was this student bullied and wants revenge? Does this student have ADHD and acts impulsively, always mouthing off? Does the student just appear socially and emotionally immature, but has good attendance, a good family life, and this is an isolated incident?

Overall, the *threat assessment* **should assess** the *risk for threat*, describing adverse factors; as well as protective factors that mitigate against possible violence that the student might/could/can carry out at school.

When all the reports are completed, the multi-disciplinary team assembles with school administrators to discuss the results and come to some **agreement as to the level of risk and potential threat.**

Recommendations should include plans to minimize future threats and should be clearly designated in the assessment summary; i.e. seek individual psychotherapy with an outside therapist; get a psychiatric evaluation to rule out suicidal ideation; refer to the office of student leadership for disciplinarian action and/or expulsion, etc.

I know of a situation where one particular school administrator, who was well trained, utilized a National School Safety Center Checklist titled " the characteristics of youth who have caused school-associated violent deaths" as the sole deciding factor in their school's decision making process for risk assessment. He alone interviewed the student, spoke to the parents, and then filled out the checklist.

Based on his impression about the student's level of risk, he then made a unilateral decision about what to do with the student. For some reason this procedure just does not strike me as comprehensive, multi-disciplinary, or professionally appropriate. Just think of the liability issues should something go sideways! This was also not the official School Board's approved plan for assessing and managing risk! He places himself in great legal jeopardy taking on the sole responsibility for risk assessment.

There is no magic list of traits or characteristics. No one has a crystal ball. **Human behavior is complex and unpredictable**. We can only avail ourselves with the best research and have a multi-disciplinary plan of action that is comprehensive. What I mean by this is**, no one person or professional has "THE ANSWER" when it comes to assigning level of risk.**

I am sure when John Hinckley's Psychiatrist first saw him in therapy, he did not feel he was at risk for shooting President Reagan, but... well that is another story all together. You cannot read a person's mind and patients frequently, often, lie to their therapists!

I offer the following text "Risk for Harm Categories" by Dr. Kris Mohandie, Ph.D., as a guide to the school's threat assessment team in determining a student's level of threat and range of risk. It is one of the many that researchers have provided for clinicians, school personnel, and community law enforcement offices.

The idea of **a risk hierarchy** is that it **assigns "realistic degrees of risk".** There is no black or white "yes "or "no" answer to the question about how much of a risk a student is. **There is a spectrum of risk. A range of risk. A level of risk.** Some people have a hard time living in this quagmire of risk assessment, but it is all there is realistically.

CAVEMAN WISDOM: "Intolerance of ambiguity is the mark of an authoritarian personality". By: Theodore Adorno.

The risk hierarchy is from the book by Dr. Kris Mohandie, Ph.D. titled "**School Violence-Threat Management: A Practical Guide for Educators, Law Enforcement, and Mental Health Professionals**". *(There is also a good discussion about the warning signs –Behavioral and Physical Clues. (look it up)*

Dr. Mohandie is a police psychologist who has worked for federal law enforcement organizations including LAPD's Threat Management Unit. He recently developed and implemented a model school violence prevention and intervention-training program for the city of Los Angeles School System.

Another good book on this subject is "**Violence, Risk and Threat Assessment": A Practical Guide for Mental Health and Criminal justice Professionals**" by Dr. J. Reid Meloy, Ph.D., also with Specialized Training Services. *(In this book there is a good discussion on risk enhancing factors and risk-reducing factors. (look it up).*

Remember, stabilizing factors are as important as the risk factors. When the school risk assessment is over, you will be left with the obligation to develop a risk-reducing plan of action; sort of like a **Behavior Intervention Plan/BIP**.

In my opinion these books offer the reader an excellent resource guide; key point to be made here, it is a guide, not a black and white answer to being able to perfectly measure threat level/risk. Remember, I do not see the focus of this guidebook to give you all the answers. The book would be too long and you could not memorize it all if you tried. I hope to whet your appetite for more information and knowledge, and get you researching these topics on your own. There is so much to learn, and so little time, so get cracking!

Risk for Harm Categories

By: Kris Mohandie, Ph.D

Category 1: Imminent Risk for Harm

Individual is, or is very close to, behaving in a potentially dangerous way to self or others. Examples include "detailed" threats of lethal violence, suicidal threats, possession or use of firearms and other weapons, serious physical fighting, etc. Most of these individuals will qualify for immediate hospitalization or arrest.

Category 2: High Risk for Harm

An individual that displays significant early warning signs, has significant existing risk factors, or has experienced precipitating events, and has few stabilizing factors in their life. May not qualify for immediate hospitalization or arrest at present, but requires referrals for needed services and active case management.

Category 3: Moderate Risk for Harm

Individual has displayed some early warning signs and may be exhibiting risk factors or a recent precipitating event, but also does have some stabilizing factors present. There may be evidence of internal or emotional distress (depression, social withdrawal, etc.) or of intentional infliction of emotional distress on others (bullying, intimidation, seeking to cause fear, etc.)

Category 4: Minor Risk for Harm

An individual who displayed minor early warning signs, but assessment reveals little history of serious risk factors or dangerous behavior. Stabilizing factors appear to be reasonably well established. There my be evidence of the unintentional infliction of emotional distress on others.

Category 5: Low/no Risk for Harm

Upon assessment it appears that there is insufficient evidence for any risk for harm. Situations under this category can include misunderstandings; poor decision-making; false accusations form peers (seeking to get other peers into trouble).

CAVEMAN WISDOM: "A common mistake that people make when trying to design something completely foolproof is to understand the ingenuity of complete fools".
By: Douglas Noel Adams.

CAVEMAN WISDOM: "The thing that's important to know is that you never know". By: Diane Arbus.

CHAPTER 3

IDEA-**I**ndividuals with **D**isabilities **E**ducation **A**ct

The SSW and Special Education

Public Law 94-142. Learn it. Memorize it. There will be a test. Not a written test, but a competency test. You will be dealing with IDEA a lot as a School Social Worker, probably on a daily basis. It is important for you to understand its regulations and provisions.

There are 14 types of student disabilities covered under IDEA- (*look it up*). You will most likely be in Special Education Committee (SEC) meetings two or three days a week. Many SEC meetings last 4 hours or more and screen new referrals, as well as conducting triennial reviews, and determining eligibility for those students who have been evaluated.

IDEA was originally enacted by Congress in 1975 to ensure that children with disabilities have the opportunity to receive a **free appropriate public education**, just like other children. The law has been revised many times over the years. The most recent amendments were passed by Congress in December 2004, with final regulations published in August 2006 (Part B for school-aged children) and in September 2011 (Part C, for babies and toddlers). So, in one sense, the law is very new, even as it has a long, detailed, and powerful history.

More than 6 million children with disabilities receive special education and related services in our schools each year. Having a disability does not automatically qualify a student for special education services under the IDEA.

To be eligible for special education services, the disability must result in the student needing additional or different services to participate in school.

IDEA defines a child with a disability "as a child... with **autism**, an **intellectual disability**, **hearing impairment** including deafness, **speech or language impairments**, **visual impairment** including blindness, **deaf-blindness**, **serious emotional disability**, **orthopedic impairment**, **traumatic brain injury**, **other health impairments**, **specific learning disability**, **multiple disabilities**, and **developmental delay**.

Children with disabilities who qualify for special education services are also automatically protected by Section 504 of the Rehabilitation Act of 1973 and under the Americans with Disabilities Act (ADA). However, all modifications that can be provided under Section 504 or the ADA can be provided under the IDEA if included in the student's IEP.

Students with disabilities who do not qualify for special education services under the IDEA may qualify for accommodations or modifications under Section 504 and under the ADA. Their rights are protected by due process procedure requirements.

Special Education committee (SEC) meetings are called into action to screen any student who someone has referred because they suspect the student may have a disability that is adversely impacting the student's academic performance or participation in the academic program. The screening SEC must determine if the suspicion is significant enough to warrant a comprehensive evaluation. If so, the SEC initiates a comprehensive assessment, with parental permission.

The team has 65 working/business days to complete all of the assessments and meet in an eligibility meeting to determine if the student qualifies for special education services.

The SEC team must determine and document that 3 eligibility criterion are met:
(1) there is documented evidence that the student does indeed manifest one of the 14 types of disabilities; (2) that there is documented evidence that the disability is severe enough to cause an adverse impact on his/her academic performance or participation in the academic program; and, (3) that a written individualized education plan (IEP) for specialized instruction is necessary in order for the student to make adequate academic progress commensurate with his/her cognitive abilities.

If any of the three-eligibility criterions are not documented, the team may decide the student is not eligible for special education services.

EXAMPLE:

A 16-year old student is making As, Bs, and Cs despite being severely depressed. He attempted suicide on three different occasions; by attempting to hang himself at home; by running into an oncoming car near his house; and once by obtaining a gun and calling 911 threatening to shoot himself.

This student's mother went before the SEC screening committee requesting an evaluation and it was recommended by the SEC that he be evaluated. At the eligibility meeting, he was indeed found to manifest a severe emotional disorder, however, eligibility criterion (2) and (3) were not met. The student was not found to be eligible for special education services.

The student had no history for depressed or bizarre behavior in the school setting. He had fair-good social relationships with peers and did well academically. There were no discipline concerns at school. His attendance was good, except for medically excused absences (hospitalization for auto accident and hanging attempt). If the parent had not referred the student to the SEC and asked that he be evaluated, none of his teachers, or school administrators, would have had any idea what was going on with this student.

The parent appealed that decision and asked for a second evaluation by new evaluators, which was approved. The second evaluation documented similar results. The SEC team was also heard before a panel of administrative judges. The same decision was reached.

The student was definitely emotionally disturbed, but somehow, his symptoms were never manifested in the school setting, and never resulted in an adverse impact on his academic performance or participation in the academic program. Therefore, he did not require academic remediation to achieve adequate academic performance and was not eligible for special education services.

What do you think? Was this a good decision? Was this decision in the best interest of the child? Was the decision lawful and in full compliance with IDEA?

Keep in mind that this special education law mandates that in order for a student to become eligible for IDEA services, some type of disability must have an adverse impact on academic performance and/or their participation in the academic program. The academic disability must be severe enough to require specialized (remedial) instruction in order for the student to make adequate progress.

In the case above, the student was capable of maintaining **adequate**, **not necessarily maximum**, peer group social relationships and grades. Evidence suggested adequate academic performance and overall academic progress throughout the school year.

Did the student require psychiatric care? Absolutely, but the school system is not obligated, nor authorized, to provide such medical/psychiatric service. Did the student need to see a therapist? Absolutely, but School Psychologists and SSWs are not authorized, or licensed, to provide the type of psychotherapy this severely depressed 16-year old with multiple suicidal attempts requires.

Bottom line, special education is not for all students with problems. There are specific laws, regulations, and eligibility criterion that must be met. There are other community resources that most SSWs know about that can meet the needs of those students who do not qualify for special education services. Can you think of any community resources that might be appropriate for the parents and the 16-year old student in the above example?

CAVEMAN WISDOM: "There is nothing worse than a brilliant image of a fuzzy concept".
By: Ansel Adams.

IDEA
Read it, learn it, and know it.

Below is a good guide to use when trying to differentiate between a Serious Emotional Disturbance. It has been my experience that there is more confusion and hence, more conflicted discussion, at SEC meetings and 504 meetings about the seriously disturbed student, and whether their symptoms are significant enough to qualify for eligible services. The following checklist is very enlightening. It specifically reviews the IDEA's (5) criteria for SED.

SED Definitions/Criterion for IDEA Eligibility
"The Differential Test of Emotions and Conduct Problems"
Slosson Publishing Co.
Edward Kelly, Ed.D.

Criterion (1): **"An inability to learn which cannot be explained by intellectual, sensory, or health factors".**

This is most specifically met when the student indicates significantly discrepant achievement performance due to **anxiety**, and/or reality distortion based causes exhibited by such conditions as:
   a. Disorders in thinking, reasoning, and/or perception suggestive of schizophrenia deterioration.
   b. Pervasive depressive symptoms affecting school performance
   c. Anxiety disorders affecting school performance including school phobic reactions
   d. Obsessive-compulsive personal achievement standards, which negatively influence school performance.

Criterion (2): **"An inability to build or maintain satisfactory interpersonal relationships with peers and teachers".**

This is most specifically met when the student engages in actions or behavioral patterns that suggest self-devaluation in relation to significant others through:

   a. Consistently anxious or fear-driven avoidance of meaningful social and/or school interactions with others
   b. Withdrawal, isolation, and/or bizarre interactive patterns suggesting symptom behaviors characteristic of schizophrenia. depression, social phobic reactions, obsessive-compulsive addictive states, etc.
   c. The consistent seeking of excessive approval of others through abusive, self-humiliating and/or immature actions.
   d. The seeking of negative attention by being ostracized, punished, humiliated, and/or hurt by others.

Criterion (3): **"inappropriate types of behaviors or feelings under normal circumstances"**, is most specifically met when the student exhibits inappropriate actions or feelings emanating from gross self-devaluation, severe anxiety states, and/or reality distortion. Such actions or feelings would include:

a. Self-destructive, catastrophic reactions to routine occurrences.
b. Hallucinatory behaviors-student describes hearing, seeing, or experiencing things that do not occur (i.e. can not be verified as real).
c. Delusions-student believes and/or acts out grossly unreal self/other perceptions (delusions or persecution, grandeur, grossly exaggerated self-importance in relation to others, jealousy, morbid health and/or body image preoccupations, etc.)
d. Extreme self-withdrawal not attributed to learned family patterns.
e. Excessive preoccupation with fantasy life, including relationships with imaginary others and corollary exclusion of normal peer interactions.
f. Bizarre non-purposeful emotional responses and actions in common social or academic situations (i.e. consistently inappropriate manic, laughing, crying, rage state behaviors, etc.) without apparent cause or motivation.

Criterion (4): **"A general pervasive mood of unhappiness or depression".** This is most specifically met when the student engages in such behaviors as:

a. Rage state behaviors, including aggressive acts, which suggest abnormally non-purposive self-destructive and/or randomly impulsive motivations (e.g. not seeking attention, power, money, social status among peers, revenge, etc.)
b. Consistently expressed feelings of guilt, moral worthlessness, self-reproach, or gross inadequacy.
c. Recurring expressions suggesting obsessions with death, being dead, committing suicide, or similar morbid preoccupations.
d. Observed chronic mood swings of extreme unhappiness, prolonged crying episodes without grief motivation or depression.
e. Depressive concomitants, including inability to make even simple decisions, total loss of interest, or pleasure in previously valued activities, unusually slowed thinking and actions, flatness of affect, etc.

Criterion (5): **"A tendency to develop physical symptoms, pains, or fears associated with personal social or school problems".** This is most specifically met when the student's physical symptoms, pains, or fears emanate from gross self-devaluation and/or persistent anxiety states, as evidenced by:

a. Consistent physical symptoms without demonstrated organic cause, which suggest an anxiety state etiology (e.g. chronic stomachaches, migraine headaches, dizzy spells, fainting, etc.) related to school performance.
b. Severe somatic conditions (ulcers, colitis, asthmatic reactions, etc.) demonstrably aggravated by the student's inability to appropriately cope with personal, social, or academic stresses).
c. Persistent, irrational fears and/or phobic reactions focusing upon specific objects, activities, situations, or individuals that result in socially disabling avoidance behaviors.

d. Consistent preoccupations with irrational fears or morbid beliefs (e.g. fear of impending catastrophes affecting self or family, belief that everyone hates them, fear of growing up or of not succeeding in school.

CHAPTER 4

SECTION 504 PLAN - part of the Americans with Disabilities Act, Amendments Act of 2008.
The SSW and Section 504

Special education means a student requires remedial education and accommodations in order for the student to be able to make adequate academic progress. If a student only needs classroom **accommodations** to be academically successful, but **not academic remediation**, maybe the student needs a 504 plan.

Do you know what *ADA* stands for? *Do you know what ADAAA stands for? What is a 504 plan? How is an ADA section-504 plan different from and IDEA special ed plan? (look it up).*

In enacting the **Americans with Disabilities Act of 1990 (ADA**), Congress intended that the Act "provide a clear and comprehensive national mandate for the elimination of discrimination against individuals with disabilities. In enacting the ADA, Congress recognized that physical and mental disabilities in no way diminish a person's right to fully participate in all aspects of society, including school, but that people with physical or mental disabilities are frequently precluded from doing so because of prejudice, antiquated attitudes, or the failure to remove societal, institutional, and physical barriers.

The Americans with Disabilities Act, Amendment Act **(ADAAA)** of 2008, signed into law by President Bush, made changes to the definition of the term disability, and also broadened that definition. The Act retains the ADA's basic definition of "disability" as an impairment that substantially limits one or more major life activities. However, it changes the way that the statutory terms should be interpreted.

BEWARE. Ignorance is everywhere. An intelligent person does not rule out an ignorant person! Most school administrators that I have met have neither read the IDEA or Section-504 of the ADA, and those that have, have never read or even heard of the 2008 ADAAA Section-504 modifications.

CAVEMAN WISDOM: Nothing is so firmly believed as that which least is known.
By: *Francis Jeffrey*

CAVEMAN WISDOM: Ignorance more frequently begets confidence than does knowledge.
By: Charles Darwin

Under Section 504, the term **'disability'** means that a **physical or mental** impairment substantially limits one or more major life activities of such individual. Major life activities include, but are not limited to, caring for oneself, performing manual tasks, seeing, hearing, eating, sleeping, walking, standing, lifting, bending, speaking, breathing**, learning, reading, concentrating, thinking, communicating**, and working.

A major life activity also includes the operation of a major bodily function, including but not limited to, functions of the immune system, normal cell growth, digestive, bowel, bladder, neurological, brain, respiratory, circulatory, endocrine, and reproductive functions.

An impairment that substantially limits one major life activity need not limit other major life activities in order to be considered a disability. **An impairment** that is episodic or in remission **is still considered to be a disability if it would substantially limit a major life activity when active.**

The determination of whether an impairment substantially limits a major life activity shall be made **without regard to the ameliorative effects of mitigating measures.** That means ameliorative measures such as taking **medications (as in children who take medication for ADHD)**, medical supplies, equipment, or appliances, low-vision devices (which do not include ordinary eyeglasses or contact lenses), prosthetics including limbs and devices, hearing aids and cochlear implants or other implantable hearing devices, mobility devices, or oxygen therapy equipment and supplies, etc.

The ADAAA provides that impairments that are episodic or in remission are to be "assessed in their active state", not in their remission state!

I have heard administrators, and other members of the 504 committee, tell a parent that before they will find a student with ADHD eligible for a section 504plan they want that child to be on medication first to see if that solves their learning/academic/behavior problems!

This is very dangerous and contrary to the law. First, you can't make a parent see a doctor, get a diagnosis, or to put a child on medication; for any reason. And, no 504-committee member should even be discussing medications whatsoever.

On the other side of the coin, just because someone is considered to have an impairment or comes with a prior diagnosis from a reputable source of impairment such as ADHD, seizures, or severe diabetes does not mean they automatically qualify for a 504 plan. The ADHD, diabetes, or seizure disorder symptoms must result in an impairment that limits a major life activity **when active.** Remember, you are not considering the mitigating effects of medications, but the active state of the disease when not under control. (ADAAA of 2008).

A disability shall not apply to impairments that are transitory and minor. A minor impairment is considered to be transitory when the expected duration is 6 months or less.

What about the student who has a documented history of having several seizures per day, many of which occurred at school, but with medication, there is only one or two seizures per month?

What about a diabetic student who requires insulin shots and sugar monitoring at school multiple times per day? Without daily insulin injections and sugar monitoring supervised by the school nurse, the student would lapse into diabetic crises. Do these types of students warrant 504 plans?

What about the student with ADHD who takes medication and usually does well? What if there have been several times he has forgotten to take his medication, or the side effects were too severe for him to continue with meds, and he could not follow the Teacher's directions, listen attentively, focus or concentrate, or complete most of his class work? Is he eligible for a 504 plan?

The ADA, Amendments Act of 2008 (ADAAA) widened the eligibility criteria for students being considered for a 504 plan. Schools can no longer say " because Johnny does so well on his medication, they do not qualify for a 504 plan". Is there documentation that there are times when the student forgets to take his medication, and when he does, he has a terrible day at school, requiring various teacher and guidance counselors to get involved and provide accommodations to get the student back on track?

Is taking **Ritalin for ADHD, or Insulin for diabetes, or Tegretol for seizures considered to be a "mitigating measure"**? (look it up).

CHAPTER 5

THE SOCIO-CULTURAL AND DEVELOPMENTAL HISTORY.

Arguably, writing a social history report is one of the most important job duties that a School Social Worker must perform. It is as much an art as a skill. It takes a great deal of executive functioning skills to complete this task professionally, successfully, and competently.

Sure, you might minimize it and down play the importance, but that would be a gross misunderstanding of its importance to the comprehensive assessment process. Next to the School Psychologist's evaluation, the social history is important because it not only complements their results; it also helps to explain the school psychologist's results.

EXAMPLE: Let's imagine J's parents have complained for years that their son needed special education services, but because he made a few B's, but mostly C's and D's in all his subjects, the teachers did not feel he had a real learning disability. They mostly categorized him as just being "slow" and "unmotivated".

A comprehensive assessment is, however, finally agreed to after two years of J's parents continuously hounding the teachers. The School Psychologist tests this 12-year old student and his Full Scale IQ is 78. Most of his academics are also commensurate with his cognitive ability, but some are elevated and in the average range. There is no explanation for the discrepancy between academic subjects, so the SEC team decides there is no learning discrepancy and no evidence to support a learning disability.

Such a profile could easily be considered to be a "slow learner profile", which is not a learning profile that is eligible for special education services. Now, let's add in information from the social history. The child's early developmental milestones were all age appropriate, if not a bit advanced. He learned to speak and communicate quickly; walking at 10 months and talking in short sentences by 18 months. His parents always felt he was very smart and he took to reading easily. He used to love going to school and his teachers loved him and praised him for his good grades all through most of elementary school.

The medical history revealed that he suffered a severe head concussion at age 9 1/2 and temporarily lost his previously acquired language and communication skills. This account of a Traumatic Brain Injury (TBI) is documented by medical records. A review of his report cards shows that in kindergarten through the fourth grade, his achievement was average to above average.

After the TBI, his personality changed and he appeared cognitively slower, anxious, and moody which was reported by his parents to be very different from his personality and cognitive functioning prior to the TBI. His middle school teachers, who had no prior knowledge of his TBI, just thought he was a typical middle school student; moody and a bit slow.

Is it now possible that the SEC can consider TBI as an eligibility factor? Without the social history, he is just another slow learner who flies under the radar. In reality, he could have easily been misdiagnosed by the psychological and found to be ineligible for any assistance.

The nature of a student's learning problems are a puzzle wrapped in an enigma. The answers are often found in the **bio-psycho-social** that the SSW arrives at during the social history and parent interview. Who knows this student better than anyone else; the teacher, the psychologist, the social worker, or the parents? I'll put my money on the parents. And it's the SSW's job to investigate school learning problems with the parent and then write about the significant etiological findings in a "social history" report.

Let's look at how to write a good, mind blowing social history. Anyone can fill in an open answer questionnaire. That is not appropriate. You have to know how to dig at underlying information, and not settle for just a true-false, open-ended answer. After the identifying information, a typical social history report should include the following headings.

*REASON FOR REFERRAL:

My typical introductory paragraph reads like this:

The above referenced student was referred by the Special Education Committee (SEC) at __School__ for a comprehensive assessment to rule out the possibility that a *__specific learning disability in reading,__ and/or and **Attention Deficit Hyperactivity Disorder** might be having an adverse impact on his/her academic performance. (*You have to specify in the SEC screening what the specific disabilities are that you suspect; i.e. specific learning disability, ADHD, Autism, Emotional Disability, Other Health Impairment secondary to a Seizure Disorder, etc. etc.).

*METHOD OF ASSESSMENT:

This writer met with the above referenced student's biological parents, Mr. and Mrs. __name__, in their home located at 1234 Sunny Side Blvd, Sunnyside, California on __date__. Pertinent family, social and developmental background information was obtained at that time. A review of the student's cumulative educational record and special education file was also performed. Pertinent medical records from Dr. __name___, MD were also provided and reviewed.

*FAMILY COMPOSITION AND DYNAMICS:

FAMILY COMPOSITION:

The socio-cultural history is usually conducted with a primary care giver, the biological parent(s) or legal guardian(s); whoever are responsible for the child's day-to-day welfare. Sometimes parents prefer the interview to be conducted at the school, or their place of employment, or even during their lunch hour at a local fast food restaurant.

These were all ok by my school division's policies. But generally speaking, the interview should take place in the student's primary residence. You get to verify if they do indeed, live in the correct school zone; and, you get to assess the habitability and suitability of the home environment. This is not always possible however, and in my opinion, one should not make it a big deal if it is conducted elsewhere. Most parents work and have very unforgiving bosses that don't like their employees to take time off.

Once involved with the special education process, a parent will attend, at the very least, the following different appointments that are held at the school: parent-teacher conference, support team conference, SEC screening meeting, SEC eligibility meeting, IEP meeting. Parents are required to spend a lot of time going to meetings and may miss a great deal of work, which may adversely affect their job security. So be understanding and tolerant.

What could be easier to write and report on than family dynamics, right? ....."Johnny lives with his biological parents, paternal grandfather, and three siblings in the paternal grandfather's home". Done, right? It is a bit more complicated than that and the additional information could shed significant light on why the student is having problems at school.

Don't forget to confirm: Parents/guardians names; names of everyone who currently lives in the same residence with the student; their current address (school zone) and phone numbers (school emergency contacts); the parent's ages; the date they were married, separated, and/or divorced; number of marriages; the biological parent's formal education and occupations; the nature of the parental child caring philosophy, and if they parent in similar or dissimilar manners.

If the parents are divorced, things get complicated. What is the custody arrangement, who has physical and non-physical custody? In their opinion, was the divorce traumatic? In their opinion, how did the divorce and custody affect the child? Describe any behavioral changes. How is the child adjusting to the custody arrangement? Can you think of anything else?

And remember, you will need to **interview both parents**. If the divorce was acrimonious, interview them separately. I cant tell you how many SEC meetings have blown up when only one parent was interviewed, usually the one with physical custody.

You MUST hear from both parents, even if one lives in a different state, or is in jail, it is mandated by law that both parents be interviewed if they both have joint custody.

When siblings are described, ask about their sleeping arrangements; ....Johnny sleeps in a room with ___ and ___, but Jenny has her own room. The SSW needs to be able to assess residential habitability and suitability, and the nature of living arrangements; i.e. say there are five siblings and two parents sharing a two-bedroom apartment. What is the bedroom arrangement for male and female siblings; ask about the ages of siblings, nature of sibling rivalry and relationships, physical and mental health of all family members, available study areas and quiet areas to do homework, etc.

Don't forget to ask about, and consider, if there is a history of **sleep deprivation**? Does the teenager that the elementary school student shares a room with stay up all night playing video games? He then goes to school tired: he can't concentrate or focus, and frequently falls asleep in class. That goes for the teenager as well! Is their insomnia? Is their apnea/snoring? Are there times the student falls asleep during the day (on the week-end)? If so consider narcolepsy/ catalepsy.

What are the current relationships with extended family members (grandparents, the mother's boyfriend and/or father's girlfriend, etc.)?

FAMILY DYNAMICS:
Family dynamics can be very complicated. You will rarely hear the truth. Truth is always predicated on perspective anyway. So in reality, there are two truths. The parent, whoever is the informant, may wish to paint an "overly good picture", or, an "overly bad picture". Be alert, and be careful and sensitive in your report writing about this information. It is better to use generalized statements rather than scandalous specifics. Remember the specifics are often severely biased and prejudicial.

EXAMPLE:
If parents are divorced, are there ongoing court hearings and hostile court battles over property and the children, etc.? For how long have the court hearing been going on?

If the mother of the student has sole physical custody of the child, but both parents share joint custody, you have a legal obligation to interview the non-custodial parent as a social history informant. The non-custodial parent still has full **legal rights** to your report, **and all information in his son's cumulative educational record and the special education files.**

You may want to set up two separate interviews, as mentioned above. When only one parent provides information, and there is a hostile parental relationship, be extremely careful what you say about each parent, their marital dynamics, and the reason for the divorce. Be extremely careful how you write about the divorced parents in your social history. There are consequences for offending one or the other parent who hears you read that report in front of a table full of strangers at the SEC meeting.

One or both have been traumatized by the divorce, don't make then SEC meeting traumatic as well. After all, the SEC meeting and the social history are about the student with a suspected learning problem, and not the acrimonious parents.

If there is a report of spouse abuse by the mother of the student whom you are interviewing, be careful how you phrase it in your report. Get her/his permission first; otherwise ask them if you can just describe it as "significant domestic conflict" or "significant marital discord". They may have a "legal right" to their marital privacy.

But, I am sure that like me, you feel a professional obligation to include this information in the social history. **BEWARE: Try to remain a neutral observer and reporter**. Try to describe what the informant told you, but innocuously. You might write that…. "Mrs. X reported that there was a chronic history of ***domestic conflict*** that ultimately resulted in their separation and divorce, and she further reported that Mr. X was diagnosed with "Bipolar disorder" and took medications for that.

You might then add:…. Mr. X was not present at this social history interview, despite several attempts to contact him, and this writer has no means of confirming this information that was provided by Mrs. X regarding Mr. X ".

Or, just **leave the info out about Mr. X's Bipolar Disorder**. My colleagues and I have discussed such cases at great length. Most feel that the information is very important and should be in the social history. There could be a strong genetic link between a biological parent with Bipolar Disorder and their child's emotional problems.

Coming from a private practice background as an LCSW and LCP, my ethics training would stipulate that Mr. X has a right to his privacy and confidentiality regarding his diagnosis of Bipolar Disorder, no matter who reported it. While it is not be considered ethical misconduct for the ex-spouse to disclose this very private information, what about those of us that are School Social Workers writing it in a report based on the ex-wife's information, and being read out loud before the SPED committee!

People who are mad at other people lie about them. Or, maybe it is true. It doesn't really matter. If you had contacted Mr. X, he might have told you that he definitely did not want that information about his diagnosis in his son's special education report and file. He has that right. Would you have entered the information into the report anyway?

Ethics 101: Doesn't **Mr. X own his medical/psychiatric diagnosis and medical treatment history? Do you own your medical and psychiatric history, and do you have the right to keep it private and confidential from others? I believe we must respect his privacy and confidentiality regarding these matters,** and in this example, the School Social Worker did not get his permission to disclose his medical/psychiatric history.

Even if it is true that Mr. X has a Bipolar diagnosis, this type of information is at the least scintillating, and will blind-side the father. When he shows up (unexpectedly) at your eligibility meeting, he will "explode" and cause quite a problem for his ex-wife, the student, and the special education committee, and YOU. After all, it was your report that let the dogs out!

The SEC team also needs accurate information to make a good decision. **So be a good diplomat**. Paint an accurate picture, but use subtlety and respect both parents' rights to their privacy.

The school system does not have the authority to know every little detail about a student's parents' private life and marriage. The school system is not a court, and you are not an attorney or a Judge. Avoid blaming. Avoid personal bias. Be non-judgmental and report the facts that are necessary to shed light on the student's learning disability. No more, no less.

Again, I can't say it enough, **"choose your words carefully"**. I've been burnt, and so have almost all of my former colleagues. If you've been doing this a while, I bet you have too.

CAVEMAN WISDOM: This is when you **assimilate, accommodate, and adapt**!. Learn to write better, safer social histories. Study the NASW and SSW ethics rules and regs. about report writing and revealing the parent's private medical diagnoses.

Ask for the informant's permission as to how you will phrase something private. It will avoid a blow up in the middle of the SEC meeting or at the least, a private chewing out and an official request to amend or remove the social history that is supposed to go into the special education file with the other reports. They actually have that right if their point is factual and accurate.

At the very worst, this important family background information may be severe enough to be seen as contributing to the discussion of **"adverse family dynamics"**, and that this type of negative family dynamics may have had an **"adverse impact"** on the child and his learning. If so, the student may not be eligible for a disability under IDEA because of the socio-cultural adverse impact.

Document your attempts to contact the non-custodial parent. Document the number of efforts and what phone numbers, and addresses you tried to contact them at. If unsuccessful, you will have to prove that you made a diligent effort.

Be accurate, but be **_ethically_** and **_legally_** correct. Stay out of trouble, because in these situations, no one else has your back. It's more about how you write the report. **Convey the "essence and context" of what is important in the report, not necessarily the scintillating and nitty-gritty details**.

I always tell the parent before the interview starts, that: "I am not a Social Worker with the Department of Social Services.....I am a **School** Social Worker employed by the School Board to conduct special education social histories.... I will be asking questions about family composition and dynamics, pregnancy, birth, early childhood development, your child's medical history, as well as his current educational problems, and his social and emotional functioning".

I then stipulate "if there is anything you tell me about you or your family, that you do not want to be put in the report, tell me now, and I will either leave it out or show you how I will describe it".

Be pre-emptive; avoid defending your report in a special education committee meeting, or a court hearing, with irate parents yelling at you. Trust me, it happens, and it happens often!

EXAMPLE:

This is how it goes down in **a worst-case scenerio**: You are in an SEC eligibility meeting at your school. Those in attendance include: You (SSW), two Teachers, the Assistant Principal, "both" (divorced) parents, the School Psychologist, the Speech Therapist, and the Special Education committee Chairperson.

Everyone goes around the table and reads their reports. When it is your turn, you pass both parents a copy of your report and start to read your report to the committee. As you get into the "nitty-gritty" parts in the social history, the mother, who was the informant, reads along in silence with you. All of a sudden she accuses you, rather loudly and emotionally, of grossly misinterpreting her comments. She states that you have written a terrible and inaccurate (social history) report. She proclaims that the information you wrote about in the report is not what she actually told you.

All of a sudden, it is you, who is blind-sided. You begin to feel severely embarrassed and totally incompetent. You are sweating profusely. On top of that, the father chimes in and tells you he is taking his copy of your report to his attorney. He has not said two words all during the meeting, but now he too accuses you of gross incompetency, in addition to yelling rather loudly at his ex-spouse. The AP has to step in and ask him to leave the meeting and calm down. The meeting is postponed until this matter can be cleared up.

Just another day in the life of a School Social Worker!

You see, frequently divorced and acrimonious parents continue to be in court over child support and custody/visitation issues, which Mrs. X did not tell you about during her social history interview with you. Both parents, while divorced for over 2 years, remain very hostile towards each other, and use visitation, child custody and child support battles to get even with each other.

They also want to use your social history in court too! What is in their child's educational record and special education file is legally theirs. What you wrote in your social history is legally theirs!

You ask yourself, what did you do wrong? You wrote exactly what Mrs. X told you. You even quoted her exact words, which were quite derogatory about the student's father. What happened is, the informant, Mrs. X, may have lied to you about the ex-spouse, or at the least, exaggerated the drama quite a bit, and did not expect the ex-spouse to show up at the meeting. Now that the ex-spouse is present, she feels trapped and defensive, and diverts the blame onto you for screwing up the report!

Remember what **Leo Tolstoy says, "Happy families are all alike; every unhappy family is unhappy in its own way"**.

Don't ever forget your **family systems theory, "**don't get **triangulated** in ongoing marital and custody fights". It is very easy to take sides, when you only hear one side.

Way to go Mr. or Mrs. School Social Worker. You have been officially ordained into the profession of School Social Work. I bet none of your school social work textbooks told you about this did they? I know none of mine did.

When I did learn something new and important abut School Social Work, it was through my professional experiences "on the job", which I refer to as CAVEMAN WISDOM for your benefit. **Assimilate, accommodate, adapt.**

*MEDICAL AND DEVELOPMENTAL HISTORY:

PREGNANCY:

Review whether or not the mother suffered any significant illnesses, medical conditions, or took any medications or recreational drugs, (or other **teratogenic** influences)**(look it up)**, during the pregnancy. Was she physically abused during her pregnancy? Did she suffer any injuries? Was pre-natal care begun early?

Describe the health of the mother throughout the entire pregnancy. Was there preeclampsia, gestational diabetes, seizures, hemorrhaging, etc.

Described the length of gestation, (usually 40 weeks), and the child's birth-weight. **(Low birth weight (with a normal gestation) is considered to be less than 5.5lbs)**. Most babies weigh 6.0 to 8.0 lbs. *There are some interesting correlates with low birth weight and learning disabilities as there are with a premature births*. (look it up).

BIRTH/DELIVERY:

Describe any complications at delivery: Emergency C-section; Meconium aspiration; Placenta previa; umbilical cord compromise with fetal distress, etc. If so, was there anoxia or hypoxia (partial or complete loss of oxygen secondary to fetal distress). Anoxia can sometimes requiring immediate resuscitation. Was there a complicated breech presentation? Maternal hemorrhaging? Low Apgar scores? Physical anomalies and/or congenital birth defects? etc.

NEO-NATAL TEMPERAMENT:

This is frequently left out or minimized in many reports, and if you ask me, this is one of the most important pieces of information that we collect. Ask the parent to describe the child's temperament between birth and age 1½. Neo-natal temperament usually predicts childhood temperament, and childhood temperament, can have a high correlation with adult temperament style. Angry? Negative mood? Irritable and obstinate? Or Easy going? Optimistic? with a Euthymic mood?

Do you remember your Alexander Thomas and Stella Chess Infant Temperament research? **How about The Difficult Child by Stanley Turecki, MD? (look them up).**

Have the parent describe the infant's ability to soothe themselves; what their activity level was (hyperactive or hypoactive); was there any tactile defensiveness (ability to tolerate being touched by others, a type of *(sensory integration/sensory processing deficit.* **(look it up)** That could affect the mother's quality of holding and hugging the infant, breast-feeding, and ultimately, in severe cases, positive or negative parent-child attachment.

Ask about other **sensory integration/sensory processing symptoms** (food texture/picky eating, loud noises, clothes tags, crowds, touching messy things, toilets flushing, hugs and kisses, and being touched by others, etc.).

Sensory processing issues can ultimately result in issues with personal space, balance and coordination, fears and phobias, relationships with family and friends, and the full range of the student's activities of daily living. These symptoms mimic other types of problems that will more than likely be considered as the primary problem: e.g. Autistic Spectrum Disorders, ADHD, selective mutism, school phobia, anxiety disorders, depression, etc.

In **rare** cases, children can have mixed sensory processing called *synesthesia.* **(look it up***)*. This can result in numbers and letters having colors or odors associated with them. There are a multitude of other mixed combinations of sensory processing issues described in the literature and some could manifest as part of a learning disorder profile.

Some of these terms and disorders are just "fun facts", and rarely encountered. They are always good to know, however, as I have seen most of them on licensing tests you might take in the near future.

DEVELOPMENTAL MILESTONES:

Documenting a child's developmental milestones may (suggest) normal development, or possible developmental delays. We look for delays in a child's **physical, cognitive, language/speech, and social/emotional development.** There are plenty of *(child development charts out there. **(look it up)**.*

Don't be too OCD about any of the usual and customary developmental parameters. If a child is not walking and talking by 12-18 months, it does not mean that child is necessarily developmentally delayed. Many "normal males" don't talk until 3 years of age. They call it the ***"Einstein Syndrome".*** **(look it up).**

More often than not, an inexperienced evaluator might jump the gun and suggest a label of either "autism", or a "communication and/or language disorder". Be generous, give development a wide berth. There is a limit however, so know when delayed development does become a problem, and get to know a lot about **child development and developmental psychology. (Look it up)**

EXAMPLE:

Let's say you have just been given a comprehensive assessment to do by your school's special education committee. The subject is a 7-year old 2nd grade male.

The reason for the referral regards the Teacher's suspicion that he is manifesting a specific learning disability. During your social history, you have asked the parent about the boy's "stages of development" regarding crawling, walking, talking, sensory processing, and neo-natal temperament.

The parent states that he didn't talk until 3 or 3 ½. He also had "sensory issues" and an "odd/inconsistent eye gaze". They were always concerned about their child and told you they took him to see several learning and developmental "specialists" since the age of 2.

They were given many different opinions and diagnosis. One Psychologist even suggested that it was the onset of "Autism". He cited the child's sensory issues and his poor eye contact and lack of language as evidence to confirm his diagnosis of autism.

Now, at age 7, the parents tell you that their child "seems normal", except for trouble reading and writing. They further tell you, when you asked about his social and emotional skills, that he has always had good social skills with family members and friends, but seems a little shy.

Then you ask about the other symptoms of Autism, (because you looked them up and have a list of the most prominent symptoms for Autism in your SSW notebook that you take with you everywhere); the parents report no history for stereotyped movements, nor any limitations or preoccupations with hobbies and/or restricted interests or problems with activities of daily living. Do you still wonder if there is a language disorder or mild autism spectrum disorder?

When deciding if a child's development seems out of sync with "normal" development, it's best to give a wide berth to the time frames and symptom picture if a child's development is otherwise within the norm. *Use* ***"Occam's Razor" wisdom***.

CAVEMAN WISDOM: As Isaac Newton described William Ockham's theory, "we are to admit no more causes of natural things than such as are both true and sufficient to explain their appearances" **(look it up)**.

In any event, you are there as a School Social Worker to gather family background and child development information and facts, not to provide a medical or psychological diagnosis. When a professional gives a diagnosis, they have to be licensed in a profession that legally authorizes them to diagnose, within the limits of their educational degree and specialized training.

School Social Workers are usually not licensed by the state to provide mental health or medical diagnosis, so be careful how you analyze and summarize your results and phrase the information in your report. Are School Social Workers in your district authorized and licensed to make diagnosis? Ask someone in authority who knows the correct answer.

Even if you are an LCSW, and licensed by your state to do so in private practice, your role as a School Social Worker may limit your legal and ethical diagnostic capabilities, and you may make yourself liable to practicing outside the scope of what a School Social Worker is authorized to do according to local School Board policies and your State's Department of Education laws and regulations. Know precisely what your specific School Social Work duties and responsibilities are, and what your professional parameters entail, and do not practice outside of those parameters.

You may report that the social history information **suggests autism like behaviors**; but you cannot say the information **is indicative of autism, that is a diagnosis.**

MEDICAL HISTORY:

Describe the student's past and present medical history regarding surgeries, hospitalizations, medical conditions, treatments, medications, seizures, sleep apnea, ADHD, traumatic injuries resulting in stitches, fractures, and head concussions/traumatic brain injuries (TBI); **especially ask about head concussions and head injuries**. Ask twice, even three times. Parents sometimes forget or minimize these incidents because the doctors told them the CAT scan was normal or there was no concussion suspected.

Research on TBI is clear that even mild closed head injuries can cause long lasting symptoms from the shearing/tearing of brain neurons that doesn't show up on CT scans.

Fractures and stitches can often identify clumsy and uncoordinated children with coordination disorders and other medical/neurological disorders, and/or even child abuse.

Seizures are not as rare as one thinks. Sometimes what is described by Teachers and parents as severe ADHD is really Petit Mal/Absence Seizures. Generalized Major Motor Seizures/Epilepsy is easy to describe once it is observed. (The *Petit Mal/Absence Seizure disorder is much more subtle and complicated*. **(look it up)**.

Don't forget about sleep apnea (snoring) in children. Not so rare, and results in sleep deprivation the next day. Teachers often describe the student as exhibiting ADHD in class, or falling asleep frequently, or appearing lazy and uninterested.

Falling asleep in class, and elsewhere, could also be suggestive of **narcolepsy. (look it up).**

Know something about some rare genetic syndromes, or at least think about the possibility of a genetic syndrome when there are mixed physical anomalies and cognitive deficits with a range of unusual behaviors described. There are many web sites that describe those rare genetic syndromes; i.e. *(Turners Syndrome; Williams Syndrome; Downs Syndrome; Klinefelter Syndrome; Neurofibromatosis; Prader-Willi; etc*. **(look them up).**

Check the student's educational record for the results of the vision and hearing screening tests. These are usually found on the school physical sheet in the student's educational record. You can't really determine if a child is eligible for special education services under the learning disability category if there is a possibility that a vision or hearing problem exists. It's in the IDEA law! (look it up).

*SOCIAL AND EMOTIONAL FUNCTIONING:

Remember what the parent told you about the child's neo-natal temperament between birth and 1½; now have the parent **describe the child's personality in 50 words or less**. This often allows the parent to "think freely" in an opened ended manner about their child. Ask what they like best about their child.

Then ask what they like least about their child. It will give you an idea of the child' social and emotional strengths and weaknesses, and how the parent really feels toward the child, and the nature of the child's personality.

Describe the child's socialization skills exhibited at home and with school peers. How does the student get along with siblings? With cousins? With other extended family members?

In your mind, try to establish the child's personality style: there are several models to choose from: I like the **_Five-Factor Domain model. (look it up)._**

-**_Openness_**-_involves active imagination, aesthetic sensitivity, attentiveness to inner feelings, preference for variety, and intellectual curiosity_

-**_Conscientiousness_**-_the trait that denotes being thorough, careful, or vigilant; it implies a desire to do a task well._

-**_Extraversion_**- _Extroverts tend to enjoy human interactions and to be enthusiastic, talkative, assertive, and gregarious. They take pleasure in activities that involve large social gatherings, such as parties, and community activities._

 -**_Agreeableness_**- these individuals are perceived as kind, sympathetic, cooperative, warm and considerate.

-**_Neuroticism (think anxiety)_**- these individuals are characterized by anxiety, moodiness, worry, envy and jealousy. They are more likely than the average to experience such feelings as anxiety, anger, envy, guilt, and depressed mood. (While Neuroticism is an old, and out dated term, substitute it with the term Irritable or Anxious).

These personality **schemas (look it up)** help to give you an idea of how a student **persistently reacts** to others and interacts with their world. If you know about a better personality schema, use it.

Other examples include: the Big Five Model, Jung's Analytical Psychology model, Hans Eysenck's Three Factor model, Raymond Cattell's 16 Personality Factors, and the Myers Briggs Type Indicator.

These are to be used just as a guide to get you thinking about the child's social and emotional ability to adapt to school and life in general, and not to diagnose the child with an abnormal personality disorder!

Next, investigate the **traditional psychiatric disorders/abnormal child psychology/child psychopathology**. I use an acronym to remember a few of the major categories from the DSM-V list of mental illnesses that could describe emotional and behavior problems being observed in the school setting.

My acronym is SAD BOAT. While not comprehensive, it gets you thinking in the right direction so you don't forget to investigate the psychiatric spectrum of mental disorders.

S- Schizophrenia Spectrum; and other thought disorder symptoms of psychotic, disorganized and repetitive bizarre thinking styles
A-Anxiety Spectrum; Generalized Anxiety, OCD, Panic Disorder, PTSD, etc. Obsessive worry. Repetitive intrusive thoughts.
D- Depressive Spectrum; Major Depression, Dysthymia, etc. Unhappiness, hopelessness, self-devaluation.
B- Bipolar Spectrum; including the DSM-V **Temperament Dysregulation Disorders** of childhood. Moody with severe ups and downs; mostly irritability and hyperactivity in children.
O- Oppositional/Defiant Spectrum; to include conduct disorder when severe enough. Obstinate, mouthy, negative and frequently challenges authority figures.
A-ADHD Spectrum; inattention with and w/o hyperactivity and impulsivity. Poor executive functioning skills; i.e. planning, organizing, executing ideas, thoughts, and plans. Off task.
T- Traumatic Brain Injury Spectrum; and related problems with executive functioning deficits secondary to head injury. Possible loss of previously achieved skills. Change in personality.

Ask general questions about the child's emotional functioning and behavior. **Is the child's behavior "disturbing", "disrespectful", or "disruptive"? (The 3 D's)**

Disturbing behavior is usually emotional/psychiatric in nature.

Disrespectful behavior is usually related to conduct problems and anti-social behavior.

Disruptive behavior is typically related to ADHD or Oppositional and Defiant Disorders, or it could be the externalization of depression and/or anxiety.

Utilize the many *free rating scales* available to you on the Internet for childhood anxiety, depression, conduct problems, ADHD, etc. *(look them up).*

Once the parent has described the child's behaviors in and around the family, focus in on the emotional and behavioral problems described by teachers; i.e. poor social skills; poor impulse control with anger management problems; seems dazed and confused; talks to himself; daydreams excessively; Is disrespectful to students and Teachers; threatens others; crawls under the table when frustrated; can't/won't participate in group work with peers; draws bizarre pictures; talks in a tangential manner; his answers to your questions are always unrelated to the question.

As a School Social Worker it is better that you know what to ask others about that solicits additional and pertinent information about the child; than to simply report what others tell you they observe.

Remember to utilize a strength-based assessment of a student's social and emotional functioning. Describe their resiliency; positive personality traits-intrapersonal and inter-personal skills; positive social skills with peers and adults; ability to adapt to new situations; ability to meet new people and "chat them up" quickly; etc. Always appears happy; makes friends easily; has many friends in the neighborhood; is always honest and truthful.

Describe a student's social and emotional maturity level. Does the student have age appropriate interests and participate in age appropriate activities; does the student play on a sports team; does the student like to help younger children or older adults, etc.

*EDUCATIONAL HISTORY:

The School Social Worker should conduct a review of the student's educational record and school history. We are tasked with assisting in the investigation as to whether or not the student has been offered adequate academic instruction over the years. Ask the parent what schools the student attended since kindergarten.

Establish the continuity of attendance and geographical stability. If the parent admits that they home schooled the child for two years, but admits they really did very little academic instruction, how can you establish whether or not a child has a learning disability even though they are two years behind in math or reading!

Students, who move around a lot and transfer from school to school, have a hard time keeping up with the varied and different academic curriculums, especially if transferring from different states. In Virginia, they learn and are tested on Virginia history. In New York, they learn and are tested on New York history.

Military families tend to move frequently and experience this on a regular basis. New friends. New schools. New homes. West coast. East coast. Japan DoD schools. Guam DoD schools. It doesn't make for a very stable academic or curriculum profile. But does that necessarily mean that they did not obtain appropriate academic instruction?

Check the student's report card for a student's academic strengths and weaknesses. Look at the **citizenship and work habits categories**. Check for **excessive absences and irregular attendance.**

The teacher's educational report is the one that will usually identify the reason for the special education referral. Types of previous academic interventions should be documented as well as the student's **response to those interventions (RTI). (look it up)** There should be a well-documented history of academic interventions before a student is referred to the special education committee if the school is doing things right.

*SUMMARY:

If you know what you are talking about, this will not be a problem. When I see reports that have extra-long summaries, (most of the school psychologist reports are appalling!) to me it reflects poorly upon the writer's skill set and professional ability to synthesize professional information they should know well. It says to the SEC team that the writer doesn't really know what is going on in his/her report and is just copying everything over and over again and calling it a summary.

No one at the SEC meeting likes to hear anyone read their report for 30 minutes. **Review the important data and make conclusions**. It says you are smart and understand your data and the results of your assessment.

The SEC team will be very grateful, trust me, as there are probably five more meetings after yours and they tend to drag on and on and become meaningless. That is not good!

Formulate a summary of the above domains. **Do not create a 3-5-page repetition** of what you already stated in the social history. **Be succinct and germane, and synthesize the results** into bullet paragraphs of no more than 1 or 1 1/2 pages in length, at the most!

I had a psychology professor that actually took points off for reports that exceeded 4 pages and summaries that were longer than 1 1/2 pages. He said that if you know what you are talking about, you could easily say it in succinct sentences and short paragraphs. But if you don't know what you are talking about, you tend to copy important information from lists in books and look other stuff up just to repeat it in your report.

It takes a little practice, but once accomplished, it is an easy thing to do. You just have to train your brain and learn to think and write in a different way. Once accomplished, others will frequently comment on what a good report you wrote.

Force yourself to have a 3 or 4 page written report and a 1 ½ page summary and stick to it. Edit, edit, edit. Pretty soon you will fall into a rhythm and either dictate or write short reports that are informative and interesting, but still very comprehensive, in no time.

Assimilate, accommodate, adapt.

I have heard many SEC team members criticize Psychologists and Social Workers behind their backs for being too wordy in meetings; they would just read their reports word for word, and they were very lengthy to boot.

Parents cannot digest and understand a 15 page social history or psychological report, or even a 5-page summary, and then be ready to hear the other reports. And **don't read your report word for word.** You've heard others do it, and it is boring, and suggests that the reader just made the stuff up and has to read it to himself to understand it!

Many were also criticized for writing reports that nobody else at the table could understand because of the 'psychobabble" (usually it is the School Psychologist with their statements about percentiles, levels of confidence, T-Scores and stanine scores), but sometimes the SSW is at fault as well.

Many parents and teachers are just plain lost, and looked dazed and confused during the 35 minute marathon "reading". We did this assessment for them; for the student, and their parents and the teachers. It should be clear, cogent, and succinct. It should be short but very informational and also very understandable.

Here is my EXAMPLE of a Social History Summary

SUMMARY:

The socio-cultural assessment evaluates family stability and residential habitability; medical history; pregnancy and birth; developmental milestones; neonatal/early childhood temperament; social and emotional functioning; and school attendance. The School Social Worker evaluates these domains in an effort to ascertain if there is an adverse impact on a student's academic progress.

Johnny was born in Long Island, New York and moved 6 times before he was 7. He attended 6 different schools before the 5th grade. His attendance has always been excellent with no excessive absences noted. He has attended Valley Elementary School since March 3, 2013 and is currently in the 2nd grade. Johnny has not repeated any grades. He was screened by the speech therapist in the 1st grade but was not eligible for speech or language intervention services. While starting over at new schools with different curriculums, Johnny had no significant problems processing the new curriculum, or making friends, after a brief adjustment period.

His mother is a Registered Pharmacist and his father is a Commander in the US Navy stationed at San Diego Naval Base since March 3, 2013. His father's job requires frequent geographical relocations approximately every two years. Mrs. X's job is over by the time Johnny is out of school and parental supervision is always consistent. As a Pharmacist, she is able to obtain new employment whenever they move.

Mr. and Mrs. X were married in 1992. It is the first marriage for both. Family relationships were reported to be close, stable, and secure. There is no report of significant family problems or crises. The family currently enjoys a stable military socio-economic lifestyle. The family resides in a 3 bedroom home with adequate space, and is felt to be conducive to a nurturing home environment. They have lived at their current residence since March 3, 2013. The neighborhood is considered to be safe with plenty of playgrounds and Johnny makes friends easily.

Johnny's pregnancy and birth were complicated by gestational diabetes and preeclampsia. He was born at 34 weeks weighing 5lb 6oz. Delivery was otherwise uncomplicated. No congenital defects were reported. Apgar scores were thought to be between 9 and 10 across all intervals. Mother and child were released after a 3-day uneventful hospital stay.

Neo-natal temperament was described as easy. Developmental milestones were reported to be inconsistent. While Johnny crawled at 6 months and walked at 16 months, he did not talk or develop any verbal language until 3 ½ years of age. He was evaluated at the Walter Reid Army Hospital Pediatric Clinic to rule out developmental delays at age 2. There were several diagnoses being proposed by various professionals between age 2 and the present that included: Mild Autism, Developmental Language and Communication Disorder, and Selective Mutism.

At the present time Johnny's parents report that he manifests a full range of age appropriate interests and activities. He plays community league soccer and baseball. He has several friends in the neighborhood that he plays with regularly and appropriately.

There were no verbal or non-verbal social or communication deficits reported. His communication skills with family members and same age peers are reported by his parents as typical for a 7 year old.

Mr. and Mrs. X describe Johnny as a generally happy and content child who is socially outgoing at present, albeit it was not always like that. He currently exhibits no behaviors that would suggest significant depression, anxiety, oddities of behavior, obsessions, fears, phobias, or aversions, although he did at an earlier age between 2-3 1/2.

There is no report of any previous hospitalizations or surgeries. Johnny is reported to be in good physical health experiencing no chronic illnesses or diseases. He takes no medications on a regular basis. His vision and hearing are reported to be normal. Johnny sleep cycle is from 9:00 pm to 6:00 am and is sound without disruption or disturbance.

There is one report of a traumatic injury when he was 5 years old. He was hit in the back of the head by a child swinging a baseball bat at a baseball game. He never lost consciousness, but did complain of a severe headache. There were no visual or balance problems reported. He went to the local hospital emergency room and the CT Scans were reported to be normal. There was no abrupt personality change or regression in previously learned cognitive skills after the incident according to his parents.

His parents state they no longer worry that Johnny might be Autistic, but report that he continues to exhibit problems with reading and writing. They wonder if he might have a learning disability.

This report is submitted to the Valley School special education eligibility committee in hopes of assisting them with their decision as to what, if any, special education services may be warranted at this time.

Jim Social Worker, MSW

Jim Social Worker, MSW
School Social Worker
jss@valleyschools.com

CAVEMAN WISDOM: "An educated person is one who has learned that information almost always turns out to be at best incomplete, and very often false, misleading, fictitious, mendacious-just dead wrong". By: Russell Baker.

CAVEMAN WISDOM: "The trouble with life isn't that there is no answer, it's that there are so many answers".
By: Ruth Benedict.

CHAPTER 6
Ethics and Confidentiality.

This can be a very complicated subject. Ethics has been explained to me by numerous lawyers and NASW training specialists as a quagmire; and it is always prefaced with "It Depends". I will probably not answer any of your questions, but rather leave you with more questions than you had before you read this.

There is no black or white answer to most ethics questions. Be sure to read your **NASW ethics guide** *and SSW ethics guide. (You can get a free copy off the NASW website) (look it up)*

Here is my simplistic explanation. It is probably not the final answer, and it may not even hold up in court, but this is what the **Social Work in** *Education Magazine printed in 1992* said in their article titled *"Confidentiality and the School Social Worker.*

* Ethics is a branch of philosophy that "deals with the question of what actions are morally right and how things ought to be".

*Consequently, Social Work ethics is a very personal study. No two individuals will make the same mistake in the same way, or reach the same conclusions, as each person's value base and range of personal experience will be different.

* For the School Social Worker, **the client is the student**.

* Therefore **the duty of confidentiality is owed to the student**.

* In the course of providing services to the student, the School Social Worker often functions as the liaison between school, home, and community. Although these entities are sources of information about the student, and may have legitimate interests in the child's best interests, and may be affected by and involved with the actions of the student, this involvement does not elevate these entities to the status of clients of the School Social Worker.

* These other entities and individuals with whom the School Social Worker works with are generally not bound by any ethical obligations.

* Ethical decision-making, regarding confidentiality in the school setting, is greatly simplified by remembering that the student is the client.

To complicate matters even more, custody issues really cause interesting issues. This type of scenario occurs every day. How should you proceed with setting up a parent interview to do a social history if a student's parents are divorced; physical custody belongs to the biological mother who lives in your city, but the non-custodial father retains parental rights and joint custody, but lives out of the city? Should the biological father be apprised of the need for a social history? Should he be invited to the SPED screening and eligibility meetings and IEP meetings? According to IDEA, the answer is yes.

The answer to these questions depends on what is in the best interest of the child; and what state law says. Every state has their own laws and they differ from state to state.

EXAMPLE: Sometimes when a non-custodial parent is informed, they could make matters worse. In one case the parent with physical custody wanted their child evaluated for ADHD. It was done, and all of the professionals believed the child did indeed exhibit "severe" ADHD. When this custodial parent went to their Pediatrician to get medication, the non-custodial parent, who had joint custody and joint decision-making rights, refused to cooperate and began a nasty and hostile court battle to block the medical treatments.

I have always been told, either as an LCP, an LCSW or SSW to: document, document, document, and always consult with supervisors, colleagues, and other appropriate professionals when in doubt. Even when consulting, always maintain the confidentially of your client by not disclosing their real name or identifying information.

CAVEMAN WISDOM: Always keep your malpractice insurance up to date!

CAVEMAN WISDOM: "It is one of the maxims of civil law, that definitions are hazardous".
By: Samuel Johnson

An excellent resource is the School Social Work Association of America. www.sswaa.org. They can provide good advice and guidance.

And don't forget about **FERPA: Family Educational Rights and Privacy Act- (Look it up).** **FERPA** gives parents certain rights with respect to their children's education records. These rights transfer to the student when he or she reaches the age of 18 or attends a school beyond the high school level. Students to whom the rights have transferred are "eligible students."

SSWAA Recommendations to Guide SSW Practice

1-School Social Workers should attempt to resolve situations in which there are divided or conflicting interests in a fashion that is mutually beneficial and protects the rights of the most parties possible.

2-When conflicts of interest arise, the primary client should be assumed to be student.

3-School Social Workers should make their loyalties transparent, and consult with colleagues or their direct supervisors to consider a reassignment of responsibilities when loyalties cannot be balanced adequately.

4-School Social Workers should actively demonstrate the relevance of school social work services to the mission of education, and/or directly address situations in which the mission of social work and education are in conflict.

5-School Social Workers should ensure that all parties understand the scope of services being provided, the goal of services, and sufficient information that will enable them to support the student.

6-When another party initiates services; the School Social Worker should make every effort to secure voluntary participation of the student.

7-School Social Workers should recognize the competence of other professionals, and support multidisciplinary efforts to serve the best interests of the student.

8-School Social Workers should strive to explain the values and ethics of professional social work and their unique competencies to advance the mission of education.

9-School Social Workers should discuss confidential information only for professional purposes and only with those with a "legitimate educational interest" (FERPA, 1974).

10-Whenever possible, confidential information should be shared with the informed **assent** of the student, or the informed **consent** of the child's parent or guardian.

11-The limits of confidentiality should be discussed and negotiated with students and revisited as often as is developmentally appropriate.

12-When explaining services to students and parents, School Social Workers should include the reason why services were requested, who will receive information about the services provided, and the possible outcomes. The explanation should take into account language and cultural differences, developmental levels, and age so that it can be understood by the parent, guardian or the student.

References:

1-Family Educational Rights and Privacy Act (FERPA) of 1974, PL 93-380, 20 U.S.C. §1232g (1974).

2-Kopels, S. (2007). Student rights and control of behavior. In P. Allen-Meares (Ed.)

3-Social work services in schools (5thed., pp. 108-144). Boston; Pearson. National Association of Social Workers (1999).

4-Code of Ethics of the National Association of Social Workers. Washington, DC: Author. Raines, J.C. (2008).

5-Evidence-based practice in school mental health: A primer for school social workers, psychologists, and counselors. New York: Oxford University Press. Wesley & Buysse. (2006).

CHAPTER 7

Useful information and names of pertinent checklists for your consideration to include in your social history i.e. bio-psycho-social developmental history/assessment.

I originally planned on listing copies of several questionnaires and rating scales that have proven useful to me in my school social work student evaluations. Usually you will be involved in determining if a student has a valid emotional disorder, learning disability, social maladjustment, family crises, developmental disability, or is at risk for violence, etc.

What I have learned is two fold: (1) School Psychologists guard their domain and usually proclaim that objective rating scales, such as specific commercially published emotional and behavior questionnaires, are their specialty, and that only they have the education, training, and expertise in administering and interpreting them. This is true; they have been trained in statistics, normative versus comparative data, and standard deviations. But that does not mean a School Social Worker with an MSW does not have similar education and training. My advice, take some psychology courses and testing courses and learn about these important evaluation issues. But ask your superiors what rating scales are approved and sanctioned by your department.

Become a behavior expert. Know the difference between test results that fall "within the norm", or fall "one or two standard deviations outside of the norm". Know precisely what this means.

(2) If you are not permitted to use standardized questionnaires or rating scales, but would like to delve into a student's behavioral strengths and weaknesses more substantially, you can develop your own questionnaire and rating scales. Yes, you can develop your own! How you say? While they may not have the same "standardized " objectivity, they will have "face value" subjectivity.

After all, what is a social history? It is a subjective guided interview. In reality, if conducted properly, it is a bio-psycho-social evaluation: i.e. Bio (biological)-Psycho (psychological)-Social (social/cultural) assessment. In my professional opinion, if your social history is biologically, psychologically, and socially comprehensive, it is even more telling and predictive of a student's strengths and weaknesses that what a standardized rating scale can provide the student's parents, or the special education eligibility committee.

In the following pages, I have provided information that can help a SSW become a more competent and skilled interviewer and evaluator, starting with how to make your own **Likert Rating Scales (look it up)** about any subject matter you feel is relevant to your evaluation.

How to Make a Likert Rating Scale

Likert Scales have the **advantage** that they do not expect a simple yes / no answer from the respondent, but rather allow for degrees of opinion, and even no opinion at all. Therefore quantitative data is obtained, which means that the data can be analyzed with relative ease. However, like all surveys, the validity of a Likert Scale attitude measurement can be compromised due to the **social desirability bias**. This means that individuals may lie to put themselves in a positive light. For example, if a Likert scale was measuring discrimination, who would admit to being racist?

Offering **anonymity** on self-administered questionnaires should further reduce some of the social pressure, and thus may likewise reduce most social desirability bias. Paulhus (1984) found that more desirable personality characteristics were reported when people were asked to write their names, addresses and telephone numbers on their questionnaire than when they were told not to put any identifying information on the questionnaire.

The Likert Scale is a popular format of questionnaire that is used in educational research, especially in the field of special education. It was invented by Rensis Likert, an educator and psychologist, who advocated for an employee-centered organization.

Since the inception of this psychometric scale, there have been several versions based on the number of points provided in the scale. That is, the Likert scale can be a four-point, five-point, six-point, and so on.

The even-numbered scales usually force a respondent to choose, while the odd-numbered scale provides an option for indecision or neutrality. Below are the two Likert scales, the four-point and the five-point. Likert scales are good for rating agreement; frequency; importance and likelihood.

The Likert Item

In making questionnaires that use the Likert Scale, not just any type of question will suffice. In fact, there is a format that must be followed in formulating the questions. The questions should ask for an agreement or disagreement. Below is an example of a Likert item:

Example:
The Bush Doctrine is an effective foreign policy.
Based on the item, the respondent will choose a number from 1 to 5 using the criteria below:
1 – strongly agree
2 – somewhat agree
3 – neutral/no opinion
4 – somewhat disagree
5 – strongly disagree

There are questions that appear to be similar to the above, but are not real Likert items. Here are some examples:

Example:
How often do you visit the zoo?
1 – Never
2 – Rarely
3 – Sometimes
4 – Often
5 – Always

EXAMPLE:
My child exhibits good social skills when talking to peers.
1-Never
2-Rarely
3-Occasionally
4-Frequently
5-Very Frequently

EXAMPLE:
My child can sit still and play a game appropriately for at least 20 minutes.
1-Almost Always True
2-Usually True
3-Occasionally True
4-Usually Not True
5-Almost Never True

Example:
Describe your child's personality.
Gregarious 1 2 3 4 5 6 7 8 9 Reclusive

Example:
How old are you?
1 – Below 18
2 – 18-25
3 – 26-35
4 – 36-50
5 – Above 50
The question above is neither a Likert-item nor a Likert-type item. It is actually considered as an ordered-category item.

Example:
How informative is this article?
Very informative 1 2 3 4 5 6 7 8 9 Not informative

The above question is considered as a discrete analog scale. It is similar to the item below:
When you are putting together the target statements in the questionnaire that is supposed to follow the format of the Likert Scale, each item should be examined to determine whether it is actually a Likert item or one of the non-Likert items described here.

As you can see, you can develop questionnaires about family relations, bullying at school, interest in school, self-esteem, anxiety, depression, and many other behavioral, educational, and emotional issues.

Remember, each student is a unique mix of strengths and weaknesses. While many evaluations are focused on the student's "deficits", a student's strengths can shed just as much light on the student's abilities as an IQ test.

The IQ test is good at assessing a student's academic and cognitive strengths and weaknesses, and is used to predict academic success in the school setting. But remember, there has never been a comprehensive, unified definition of intelligence. There is emotional intelligence, artistic intelligence, musical intelligence, etc.; all informative strengths that the typical IQ test used in school settings does not assess. Be sure to consider the student as a whole, not simply an academic or behavioral deficit!

Let the School Psychologist do their job, and learn how to conduct a comprehensive social history that will blow everyone away and shed more light about the student as a whole person, with competencies, strengths, talents, and positive attributes that the psychological tests cannot begin to assess.

You can also assess pertinent biological, developmental, personality, temperament, and behavioral strengths and weaknesses, that are not otherwise evaluated, to help describe the total person.

ARTICLES OF INTEREST

The following pages contain information that I have come across and have found very interesting, and informative. The articles have enhanced my ability to perform my duties as a SSW both when discussing childhood issues with parents during my parent interviews, as well as those discussions at SEC and 504 meetings.

There is no better feeling than being an informed and knowledgeable professional. As an SSW, there are so many multi-disciplinary domains that we must develop some degree of expertise in, it is hard to keep up. Hopefully some of these articles might be of use to you in your endeavors as an SSW.

CAVEMAN WISDOM: "Any fool can know. The point is to understand."
BY: Albert Einstein

CAVEMAN WISDOM: "It is not that I'm so smart. But I stay with the questions much longer."
By: Albert Einstein

CAVEMAN WISDOM: "The more I read, the more I acquire, the more certain I am that I know nothing."
BY: Voltaire

Neo-Natal Birth Weight and the Implications of Low Birth Weight

By: Boston Children's Hospital /Harvard Medical School and the U.S. Department of Health and Human Services, Centers for Disease Control and Prevention, National Center for Health Statistics, Division of Vital Statistics, Natality public use data

I mentioned earlier how important birth weight was to the developing fetus and could be important when investing medical etiology for learning disabilities. Birth weight is the first weight of your baby, taken just after he or she is born. A low birth weight is less than 5.5 pounds. A high birth weight is more than 8.8 pounds.

Low birth weight can occur at full term too. That means the baby is born from 37 to 41 weeks of pregnancy, but exhibiting low weight. These babies may be physically mature, but small.

Complications that can occur during the newborn period include respiratory distress, jaundice, anemia, and infection. Long-term complications can include learning and behavioral problems, cerebral palsy, lung problems, and vision and hearing loss.

As a result of these risks, preterm birth and low birth weight for full gestation are leading causes of infant death and childhood disability. Babies who are born the earliest and smallest have the highest risks of morbidity and mortality. For example, infants born very preterm (less than 32 weeks' gestation) or at a very low birth weight (less than 1,500 grams: 3.3lbs) have 89 and 110 times the risk of dying in the first year of life as their full-term and non-low birth weight counterparts, respectively (see page on infant mortality).

In other words, more than half of all infant deaths occur among the less than 2 percent of infants born very preterm or at low birth weight. However, even babies born "late preterm" (34–36 weeks' gestation) or at moderately low birth weight (1,500–2,499 grams: 3.3lbs-5.5lbs) are more likely than full-term and normal birth weight babies to experience morbidity and mortality.

Preterm birth and low birth weight exact a heavy societal toll with the annual economic burden related to preterm birth estimated to exceed $26 billion, including costs for medical care and early intervention as well as lost productivity due to disabling conditions.

The causes of preterm birth are not well understood but are linked to infection and vascular disease as well as medical conditions, such as diabetes and hypertension, which may necessitate labor induction or cesarean delivery.

The majority of very low birth weight infants are born prematurely, whereas those born at moderately low birth weight include a mix of prematurity as well as fetal growth restriction that may be related to factors such as maternal hypertension, tobacco smoke exposure, and inadequate weight gain during pregnancy.

Low birthweight in newborns: Symptoms & Causes. What causes low birthweight?

The primary cause is **premature birth**, being born before 37 weeks gestation; a baby born early has less time in the mother's uterus to grow and gain weight, and much of a fetus's weight is gained during the latter part of the mother's pregnancy.

Another cause of low birthweight is intrauterine growth restriction. This occurs when a baby does not grow well *in utero* because of problems with the placenta, the mother's health or birth defects. Babies with Intrauterine growth restriction (IUGR) may be born early or full-term; premature babies with IUGR may be very small and physically immature, and full-term babies with IUGR may be physically mature but weak.

Which babies are affected by low birthweight?

Any baby born prematurely is more likely to be small. However, there are other factors that can also contribute to the risk of low birthweight. These include:

- Race - African-American babies are twice as likely as Caucasian babies to have low birthweight.
- Mother's age - Teen mothers (especially those younger than 15) have a much higher risk of having a baby with low birthweight.
- Multiple births - Multiple birth babies are at increased risk of low birthweight because they often are premature.
- Mother's health - Babies of mothers who are exposed to illicit drugs, alcohol and cigarettes are more likely to have low birthweight. Mothers of lower socioeconomic status are also more likely to have poorer pregnancy nutrition, inadequate prenatal care, and pregnancy complications — all factors that can contribute to low birthweight.

Why is low birthweight a concern?

If your baby has a low birthweight for gestation, she may be at increased risk for complications. Her tiny body is not as strong, and she may have a harder time eating, gaining weight and fighting infections. Because she has so little body fat, she may have a hard time staying warm in normal temperatures.

Because many babies with low birthweight are also premature, it is can be difficult to separate the problems due to the prematurity from the problems of just being so tiny.

In general, the lower a baby's birthweight, the greater the risks for complications. The following are some of the common problems of low birthweight babies:

*low oxygen levels at birth
*inability to maintain body temperature
*difficulty feeding and gaining weight
*infection
*breathing problems, such as **respiratory distress syndrome** (a respiratory disease of prematurity caused by immature lungs)
*neurologic problems, such as **intraventricular hemorrhage** (bleeding inside the brain) gastrointestinal problems such as **necrotizing enterocolitis** (a serious disease of the intestine common in premature babies)
***Sudden Infant Death Syndrome (SIDS)**

Nearly all low birthweight babies need specialized care in the Neonatal Intensive Care Unit (NICU) until they gain weight and are well enough to go home. Fortunately, there is a 95 percent chance of survival for babies weighing between 3 pounds, 5 ounces and 5 pounds, 8 ounces.

Can low birthweight be prevented?

Prevention of preterm births is one of the best ways to prevent babies born with low birthweight. Prenatal care is a key factor in preventing preterm births and low birthweight babies.

At prenatal visits, the health of both mother and fetus can be checked. Because maternal nutrition and weight gain are linked with fetal weight gain and birthweight, eating a healthy diet and gaining the proper amount of weight in pregnancy are essential.

Mothers should avoid alcohol, cigarettes and illicit drugs, which can contribute to poor fetal growth, among other complications.

Childhood Onset Bipolar Disorder
Pediatric Bipolar Disorder
Disruptive Mood Dysregulation Disorder
Temperament Dysregulation Disorder with Dysphoria

Childhood Bipolar Disorder, also known as Pediatric Bipolar Disorder, is often referred to as a form of bipolar disorder that occurs in children. While its existence is still a matter of some academic debate and disagreement, there is a growing body of evidence that suggests that bipolar disorder can exist in children.

Unlike most adults who have Bipolar Disorder, however, children who have Pediatric Bipolar Disorder are characterized by abrupt mood swings, periods of hyperactivity followed by lethargy, intense temper tantrums, frustration and defiant behavior. This rapid and severe cycling between moods may produce a type of chronic irritability with few clear periods of peace between episodes.

DSM-V refers to these children as exhibiting a Disruptive Mood Dysregulation Disorder, and sometimes prior to the official publication of DSM-V, was referred to as Temperament Dysregulation Disorder with Dysphoria.

Disruptive Mood Dysregulation Disorder (DMDD) is a childhood condition of extreme irritability, anger, and frequent, intense temper outbursts. DMDD symptoms go beyond a being a "moody" child—children with DMDD experience severe impairment that requires clinical attention. DMDD is a fairly new diagnosis, appearing for the first time in the Diagnostic and Statistical Manual of Mental Disorders (DSM-5), published in 2013 .

DMDD symptoms typically begin before the age of 10, but the diagnosis is not given to children under 6 or adolescents over 18. A child with DMDD experiences:
- Irritable or angry mood most of the day, nearly every day
- Severe temper outbursts (verbal or behavioral) at an average of three or more times per week that are out of keeping with the situation and the child's developmental level
- Trouble functioning due to irritability in more than one place (e.g., home, school, with peers)

To be diagnosed with DMDD, a child must have these symptoms steadily for 12 or more months.

Risk Factors

It is not clear how widespread DMDD is in the general population, but it is common among children who visit pediatric mental health clinics. Researchers are exploring risk factors and brain mechanisms of this disorder.

PEDIATRIC BIPOLAR RESEARCH

Because the current Diagnostic and Statistical Manual of Mental Disorders (DSM-V) doesn't recognize bipolar disorder occurring during childhood, there are no official bipolar symptom criteria. The DSM-V criteria for DMDD have replaced the pediatric bipolar symptom list.

Pediatric bipolar researchers have used criteria similar to that of adult bipolar disorder, requiring a child or teen to meet at least four or more of the following:

- an expansive or irritable mood
- extreme sadness or lack of interest in play
- rapidly changing moods lasting a few hours to a few days
- explosive, lengthy, and often destructive rages
- separation anxiety
- defiance of authority
- hyperactivity, agitation, and distractibility
- sleeping little or, alternatively, sleeping too much
- bed wetting and night terrors
- strong and frequent cravings, often for carbohydrates and sweets
- excessive involvement in multiple projects and activities
- impaired judgment, impulsivity, racing thoughts, and pressure to keep talking
- dare-devil behaviors (such as jumping out of moving cars or off roofs)
- inappropriate or precocious sexual behavior
- grandiose belief in own abilities that defy the laws of logic (ability to fly, for example)

Keep in mind that many of these behaviors, in and of themselves, are not indicative of a mental disorder, and could be characteristic of normal childhood development. For instance, separation anxiety, by itself, is a normal fear of being separated from one or both of the parents (for instance, attending the first day of first grade or if the parents want to go out for a night).

When thinking of a mental health disorder in childhood, **think chronicity and severity** to differentiate between normal and abnormal states.

Childhood bipolar disorder is characterized by many of these symptoms, taken together, and marked by rapid mood swings and hyperactivity. These symptoms must also cause significant distress in the child or teen, occur in more than just one setting (e.g., at school and at home), and last for at least 2 weeks.

Later in a child's development, hyperactivity, fidgetiness, difficulties making changes, and high levels of anxiety (particularly in response to separation from the child's mother) are commonly seen. Additionally, being easily frustrated, having difficulty controlling anger, and impulsiveness (difficulty waiting one's turn, interrupting others) often result in prolonged and violent temper tantrums, aspects of a normal, but difficult, childhood development.

An estimated 50 percent to 80 percent of those with COBPD have ADHD as a co-occurring diagnosis. Since stimulant medications often prescribed for ADHD (Dexedrine, Adderall, Ritalin) have been known to escalate the mood and behavioral fluctuations in those with COBPD, it is important to address the bipolar disorder before the attention-deficit disorder in such cases. Some clinicians suggest that the prescription of a stimulant for a child genetically predisposed to develop bipolar disorder may induce an earlier onset or negatively influence the cycling pattern of the illness.

While the symptoms of COBPD and ADHD may be similar, their origins differ. For instance, destructiveness and misbehavior are seen in both disorders, but these behaviors often seem intentional in those with COBPD and caused more by carelessness or inattention in those with ADHD.

Physical outbursts and temper tantrums, also features of both disorders, are triggered by sensory and emotional overstimulation in those with ADHD but can be caused by limit-setting (e.g., a simple "No" from a parent) in those with COBPD. Furthermore, while those with ADHD seem to calm down after such outbursts within 15 to 30 minutes, those with COBPD often continue to feel angry, sometimes for hours. It is important to note that children with COBPD are often remorseful following temper tantrums and express that they are unable to control their anger.

Other symptoms, such as irritability and sleep disturbances often accompanied by night terrors with morbid, life-threatening content (e.g., nuclear war or attacking animals), are commonly seen in those with COBPD but are rarely associated with ADHD.

Deficits in shifting and sustaining attention, as well as difficulties inhibiting motor activity once initiated, can strongly influence both classroom behavior and the establishment of stable peer relationships. Distractibility, daydreaming, impulsiveness, mischievous bursts of energy that are difficult for the child to control, and sudden intrusions and interruptions in the classroom are also common features of the COBPD.

Stubborn, oppositional, and bossy behavior, usually appearing between the ages of six to eight pose significant problems for parents, educators, and peers. Risk-taking, disobedience to authority figures, and the likelihood of becoming addicted to psychoactive drugs such as marijuana and cocaine also present serious concerns to those affected by a child with COBPD. Furthermore, a **high percentage of children with COBPD have co-occurring learning disabilities,** a problem that can negatively affect school performance and self-esteem.

CAVEMAN WISDOM: The new DSM-V has developed new criteria for childhood onset bipolar disorder and is calling it **Disruptive Mood Dysregulation Disorder/Temperament Dysregulation Disorder with Dysphoria.**

The term childhood "bipolar" disorder is nowhere to be seen in DSM-V, but the new DMDD diagnostic category was specifically developed to cover this controversial topic.

The DSM research group agreed on this new category because they found statistically that not all childhood bipolar studies concur that children diagnosed with DMDD progressed into adult Bipolar Disorder.

TYPES OF LEARNING DISABILITIES

VISUAL PROCESSING DISORDERS

Visual Processing involves how well a student can use visual information. When they see something, especially something complex, do they understand it quickly and easily? Can they 'visualize' things (like pictures, shapes, words, etc.) in their head? Can they remember information that they see?

Visual Processing includes:

seeing differences between things
remembering visual details
filling in missing parts in pictures
remembering general characteristics
visual-motor coordination
visualization and imagination
organization of their room, desk, etc.
art

Students with a general visual processing disability often experience most learning difficulty in the areas of **math** and **spelling** because they have trouble 'visualizing' words, letters, symbols, etc.

Specific difficulties may include:
WRITING
poor handwriting
poor spelling (cannot visualize the words)
- math
difficulty visualizing problems
difficulty with cluttered worksheets
READING
slow speed
poor comprehension
GENERAL poor organization/planning/neatness
difficulty rechecking work for accuracy
difficulty learning by demonstration
difficulty learning by video

Auditory Processing Disorders

Auditory processing involves how well a student can understand auditory information. Can they 'keep up' when people talk very fast? Can they tell voices apart easily (even on the phone)? Can they imagine the voices of familiar people in their head? Can they remember information that they hear?

Auditory Processing includes:

hearing differences between sounds/voices
remembering specific words or numbers
remembering general sound patterns
understanding even when they miss some sounds
blending parts of words together
music

Students with a general auditory processing disability usually have most difficulty with **general reading, general writing, and language (understanding and expressing)**. Specific difficulties may include:

READING

poor decoding of new words
poor comprehension
- writing
poor spelling/mechanics
poor sentence structure

COMMUNICATION

difficulty with expression
poor receptive language

GENERAL

difficulty following oral directions
difficulty learning in lectures

Sequential Processing Disorders

Sequential/Rational processing appears to be the main filing system in the brain. It involves organizing and memorizing specific bits of information including facts, figures and formulas. This is very much like a computer organizes and stores information. How well does a student remember details (like names, addresses, facts, etc.)? How organized are they?

Sequential/Rational processing includes:
Short-term memory for details
long-term retrieval of details
fine-motor coordination
finding the words you want to say or write
organization of your thoughts and materials
writing mechanics (spelling, punctuation)
reading speed/sounding out new words
attention to details
putting words and thoughts in order

Students experiencing a general Sequential/Rational processing disability often have most learning difficulties in the areas of **basic reading, math computation, expressive language, and writing mechanics.** Specific difficulties may include:
Handwriting
speed/clarity
letter reversals
spelling/mechanics
letters in wrong sequence (order)
READING
decoding (sounding out words)
speed/fluency
remembering details
attention/concentration
MATH
remembering formulas/steps
- communication
finding words for verbal or written expression
- general
planning lengthy assignments
remembering details
paying attention - easily distracted by surroundings
remembering names of people or objects
following specific directions

Conceptual / Holistic Processing Disorders

This involves looking for 'the big picture', overall patterns and underlying concepts for use in higher-order thinking, creating, and reasoning. Conceptual/holistic filing is like throwing things into boxes with very general labels.

Conceptual/Holistic (right-brain) processing includes:

memory for general themes or ideas
reasoning
spatial awareness
general knowledge
inferential thinking
estimation/approximation
conceptual understanding
creativity/inventiveness
reading comprehension
use of context
rhythm
music
art

Students experiencing a general conceptual/holistic processing disability often perform quite well during early school years but later experience much difficulty with **reading comprehension, math reasoning, and creative writing**. Specific difficulties may include:

READING

understanding irony, inferences, sarcasm
general comprehension

MATH

generalizing to new situations
story problems

WRITTEN LANGUAGE

creative writing
- communication

COMMUNICATION

general language comprehension
understanding humor

GENERAL

global/general awareness
attention - may focus too much on a specific area

Processing Speed Disorders

Processing Speed refers to how fast information travels through the brain. All LD students experience some processing speed difficulty when required to process information through their weakest processing 'channel' or 'modality'. But for other LD students, a general weakness in **processing speed** causes difficulty in all processing areas.

It is like having the brain work at 40 miles per hour when the rest of the world (and all the information) is going 55 miles per hour. Such students just can't keep up.

Processing Speed affects:

short-term memory (with time pressure)
long-term retrieval (with time pressure)
talking speed, word-finding
writing speed
reading speed
attention
reasoning (with time pressure)
general response speed

Students experiencing a general Processing Speed disability often have learning difficulties in all academic areas due to their inability to process all types of information quickly. Specific difficulties may include:

READING
reading speed
ability to stay focused while reading
MATH
completing a series of problems
WRITTEN LANGUAGE
writing speed
mechanics
clarity (with time pressure)
COMMUNICATION
delays in responding
slow, deliberate speech
word-finding difficulties
GENERAL
coping with implied or expressed time pressures
always 'a step behind'
difficulty maintaining attention to tasks
exceeding time limits during tests
trouble with social pressures to perform 'faster'

EXECUTIVE FUNCTIONING (EF) SKILLS

You will hear the School Psychologist mention EF skills frequently. They are extremely important to academic/school success. They develop over time and may not mature until around 25 years of age. The neurological area responsible for EF skills is the Pre-Frontal Cortex.

EF skill deficits are frequently noted in ADHD, Depression, Anxiety, and Mood Disorders to name a few. When considering whether or not an emotional disorder is having an adverse impact on academic performance, make sure the school Psychologist checks EF skills. There are some checklists you can use during your parent interview that the parent can fill out as well.

Since the School Psychologist is the best one to test for EF deficits, your checklists completed by the parent can **"allude to the suspicion that EF deficits reported by the parent"** **"might be a contributing factor in the student's academic problems"**.

EF refers to the overall ability to manage or regulate all of the various cognitive and emotional processes. This involves initiation, planning, organization, and execution of various tasks, as well as the ability to cope with transitions or regulate emotional responses. Weakness in this area is often associated with ADHD.

Executive Functioning skills involve:
> ability to stay focused on tasks
> ability to plan and anticipate
> organization of thoughts and materials
> ability to follow-through and complete tasks
> ability to cope with unstructured situations
> ability to cope with changes in routine
> ability to regulate emotions

Students experiencing general Executive Functioning difficulties often struggle academically with work-completion, organization, and motivation for any task which is perceived as difficult, frustrating, or simply unappealing. Specific difficulties may include:

READING
motivation when material is 'boring'
speed/fluency - skipping words or lines
remembering details
attention/concentration

MATH
difficulty seeing the 'relevance'
difficulty maintaining motivation to complete practice worksheets

GENERAL
planning lengthy assignments
remembering details
paying attention - easily distracted by surroundings
completing assignments
following specific directions
ability to keep school a 'priority'

Global OCD Scale
National Institute of Mental Health

Minimal within range of normal or very mild.
Person spends little time resisting symptoms of anxiety and impulsivity. Almost all or no interference in daily activity.

4-5-6   Subclinical OCD behaviors.
Mild symptoms that are noticeable to patient and observer, cause mild interference in patient's life and which he may resist for a minimal period of time. Easily tolerated by others.

7-8-9   Clinical OCD Behavior.
Symptoms that cause significant interference in patient's
life and which he spends a great deal of conscious energy resisting symtoms. Requires some help from others to function in daily activity.

10-11-12   Severe OCD behavior.
Symptoms that are crippling to the patient, interfering so that daily activity is "an active struggle". Patient may spend full time resisting symptoms. Requires much help from others to function.

13-14-15   Very Severe OCD behaviors.
Symptoms that completely cripple patient so that he requires close staff supervision over eating, sleeping, and so forth. Very minor decision making or minimal activity require staff support, "worst I've ever seen".

OCD Treatment Program Outline
John S. March, MD/Duke University Medical Center

1. Psycho-education about OCD with parent and child
2. Begin to externalize OCD from the patient: rename the disorder; give it a nickname ; learn to Beat Back OCD
3. Introduce the fear thermometer while developing the symptom list (YB-OCS)
4. Identify the triggers
5. Then rank and list faulty assumptions on the stimulus hierarchy sheet (Fear Thermometer)

Triggers	Obsessions	Compulsions	Fear Rating

6. Keep daily diary/journal
7. Develop rewards for beating back OCD obsessions and compulsions
   a. Begin CBT training: * reinforcing accurate info @OCD; **Cog resistance; ***self-administered pos. self -talk
   b. Three validated Tx techniques incl.:*constructive self-talk **cog restructuring ***cultivating detachment
8. Analyze catastrophic estimations of danger (Cog. Restructuring) . Look at patient's perceived responsibility for occurrence of the catastrophe. Confront the "faulty assumptions".
9. Cultivating Cognitive Detachment *(no need to avoid the triggers or participate in the rituals)* includes four simple statements: *It's just OCD again; ** my brain is hiccupping again ***these hiccups are not all that important ****I guess I should go do something else until these hiccups go away (*Talking Back to OCD)*
10. Assign E/RP homework in a transitional zone stimuli that is most likely to be successful.
11. Assign 10 min of "worry time" (satiation) to cope with mental obsessions more effectively, and teach "how to defer/eliminate the compulsions", i.e. response prevention/extinction.
12. Assign 1 minute log writing and audio taping the obsessions.
    a. Then schedule a 30 minute/per/day listening homework session of the tape. Play it over and over and over, inducing satiation and response prevention and extinction.
13. Assign new "ritual rules" (compulsion modifications) to be practiced. * delay the ritual. **shorten the ritual. ***do the ritual differently. ****do the ritual slowly.
14. Practice beating back OCD triggers and symptoms "In Vitro" in the office.
15. Increase family involvement from cheerleader to co-therapist as appropriate.
16. Celebrate success, review the tool kit, reinforce RP, provide booster sessions.
17. Reduce meds 25% every 2-3 months after 6-12 months of Rx treatment.
18. Effective CBT results in 20-30% achieving complete remission; with 5-10%l remaining quite ill and symptomatic.
19. Medication is like a dimmer switch with regard to the affective component, and is more useful with co-morbid disorders (panic disorders/social anxiety/depression) that may interfere with CBT treatment: but CBT is what corrects the OCD. In essence, CBT helps the medication, but medication alone does not achieve OCD remission! Start with CBT alone. If after 6-10 weeks the patient still has trouble resisting the obsessions and compulsions, using meds may be a good idea .In severe and difficult cases, begin both simultaneously.

Psychopathy Check List: Youth Version
PCL:YV 20 Questions
Trait Descriptions
Robert Hare, Ph.D.

Sometimes you just need to know when the hair on the back of your neck is standing up if the person who is causing this is a psychopath/sociopath.

Dr. Robert Hare, Ph.D. is one of the preeminent researchers in this area. He has developed several checklists that are worthwhile familiarizing yourself with

CAVEMAN WISDOM: "All the reading in the world cannot immunize you from the devastating effects of psychopaths. Everyone, including the experts, can be taken in, conned, and left bewildered by them. A good psychopath can play a concerto on anyone's heart strings".
BY: Robert D. Hare

CAVEMAN WISDOM: "I always said that if I wasn't studying psychopaths in prisons, I'd do it at the stock exchange".
BY: Robert D. Hare

Here are the criteria that Dr. Hare has found in his research that best describes psychopathy.

1-IMPRESSION STYLE: Interaction style is insincere and shallow. Many adolescents with this style are able to tell unlikely but convincing stories that place themselves in a good light. They are often talkative and have a tendency to ramble off topic. The may succeed in presenting themselves well and may even be quite likeable. However, they generally seem too slick and smooth to be entirely believable. They may use technical terms and jargon inappropriately to impress others. Some may be less effective at influencing your impression. Thus, they do not appear charming, but still come across as phony or superficial.

2-GRANDIOSE SENSE OF SELF-WORTH: This trait describes youth with grossly inflated views of their abilities and self-worth. They present with an attitude of superiority and may impress as braggarts. They often appear domineering, opinionated, grandiose, and arrogant. They have an exaggerated regard for their abilities and, consequently, display little embarrassment about any current problems or concern about the future. They tend to attribute any educational, family, or legal problems to external factors rather than to themselves.

3-STIMULATION SEEKING: These individuals demonstrate a chronic and excessive need for novel and exciting stimulation. They usually express a strong interest in taking chances and doing things that are exciting, risky, and challenging. They may try and use many types of drugs.

They tend to have a short attention span and frequently complain that school, work, and relationships are boring. They may comment that they need to be "on the go" or "where the action is".

4-PATHOLOGICAL LYING: Lying and deceit are a persuasive part of interacting with others. Their readiness to lie and the apparent ease with which thy carry it off (even with people who know them well) can be quite remarkable. When caught in a lie or when challenged with a contradiction, they seldom appear embarrassed, simply changing a story or reworking the facts so that they appear to be consistent with what was originally said. They have an explanation or excuse for everything. Moreover, even after repeatedly breaking their promise, and commitments to someone, they still find it easy to make new ones. They often lie for obvious reasons, but deceiving others also appears to have some intrinsic value for them. They may freely discuss and take pride and pleasure in their ability to lie.

5-MANIPULATION FOR PERSONAL GAIN: Uses deceit and deception to cheat, exploit, or manipulate others. They may carry out schemes and scams or may simply distort or misrepresent the facts for personal gain (money, sex, status, power, etc). Whereas some attempts to manipulate are elaborate and well thought out, others are quite simple and transparent. In all cases, these actions are taken with no concern for the victims. Manipulative behaviors include both criminal and noncriminal activities. The individual will describe how they "use" family, friends, or partners to achieve what they want. They may also show a predilection for using a variety of dishonest and unethical practices that are of dubious legality or that make use of loopholes in the social services and youth justice system.

6-LACK OF REMORSE: Individuals show a general lack of concern for the negative consequences that their actions, both criminal and noncriminal, have on others. They are more concerned with the effects their actions have upon themselves that about any suffering experienced by their victims or damage done to society.

They may be completely forthright about the matter, calmly stating that they have no sense of guilt, that they are not sorry for the things they have done, and that there is no reason why they should be concerned now that the matter is finished. On the other hand, they may verbalize some remorse, but in an insincere manner.

Lack of remorse may be indicated in many ways. They might fail to appreciate the seriousness of their actions (e.g. feeling that sanctions were too severe or that they were judged unfairly), they might justify their actions (e.g. blaming their victims, others or extenuating circumstances), or they might repeatedly engage in activities that are clearly harmful to others.

7-SHALLOW AFFECT: Individuals appear unable to experience a normal range and depth of emotion and, consequently, have superficial bonds with others. They appear cold and unemotional. Displays of emotion generally dramatic, shallow, and short lived: they leave careful observers with the impression that they are play-acting and that little of real significance is going on below the surface. They may admit that they are unable to experience strong emotions or that they sham emotions. Often, their emotions may not be consistent with their actions or with their situation. Sometimes they claim to experience strong emotions, yet seem unable to describe the subtleties of various affective states.

8-CALLOUS/LACK OF EMPATHY: individual attitudes and behavior indicates a profound lack of empathy and a callous disregard for the feelings, rights, and welfare of others. They are only concerned with themselves and view others as objects to be used. They are cynical and selfish. Any appreciation of the pain, anguish, or discomfort of others is merely abstract and intellectual. They are contemptuous of or indifferent to the needs of others.

9-PARASITIC ORIENTATION: Exploitation of others is an intentional lifestyle component. Such orientation may be evident in the avoidance of steady, gainful employment, while peers and siblings work at part-time or summer jobs. Instead, they may rely on family, relatives, or social assistance. A parasitic orientation may also be apparent in attempts to persuade others to fulfill their household, school, work, or social commitments (e.g. requirements of a club, team, or agency). They may achieve others' cooperation by posing as helpless and deserving sympathy and support, by using threats or coercion, or by exploiting victims' weaknesses. Their use of others in this way is not simply the result of temporary circumstances.
Rather it reflects a persistent pattern of behavior in which others are called upon to cater to their needs or discharge their responsibilities, no matter what the economic or emotional cost to the helpers.

10-POOR ANGER CONTROL: Individuals are easily angered or frustrated. They may be described as short-tempered or hot headed and tend to respond to frustration, failure, discipline, and criticism with violent behavior or with threats and verbal abuse. They take offense easily and become angry and aggressive over trivialities. These behaviors will often seem inappropriate, given the context in which they occur. The behaviors are often short-lived and these individuals may quickly act as if nothing out of the ordinary has happened.

11-IMPERSONAL SEXUAL BEHAVIOR: individuals whose sexual relations with others are impersonal, or trivial. This may be reflected in frequent casual liaisons (e.g. one-night stands), indiscriminate selection of sexual partners, and maintenance of several relationships at the same time, frequent infidelities, prostitution, or a willingness to participate in a wide variety of sexual activities. In addition, these individuals may coerce others into sexual activity with them and may engage in sexually aggressive behaviors.

12-EARLY BEHAVIOR PROBLEMS: These individuals had serious behavior problems as children (i.e. age 10 and below). These problems may include persistent lying, cheating, theft, robbery, fire-setting, truancy, disruption of classroom activities, substance abuse (including alcohol and glue sniffing), vandalism, violence, bullying, running away from home, and precocious sexual activities. These externalizing behaviors are more serious than those exhibited by most children, and they often result in complaints by other people, suspensions or expulsions from school, or contacts with the police or mental health professionals.

13-LACKS GOALS: Individuals demonstrate an inability or unwillingness to formulate plans and commitments. They tend to live day to day, to change plans frequently, and to not give serous thought to the future.
They may express little or no interest in obtaining an education or finding a steady job, and may report unrealistic aspirations with no plans on how to achieve these goals.

14-IMPULSIVITY: Behavior is generally impulsive, unpremeditated, and lacking in refection. They often do things on the spur of the moment, because they feel like it, or because an opportunity presents itself. They are unlikely to spend much time weighing the pros and cons of a course of action, or in considering the possible consequences of their actions to themselves or to others. They will often break off relationships, quit school, change plans suddenly, or leave home on little more than a whim and without bothering to inform others.

15-IRRESPONSIBILITY: Individuals habitually fail to fulfill or honor obligations and commitments to others. They have little or no sense of duty or loyalty to family, friends, employers, society, ideas, or causes. Their irresponsibility is evident in a variety of areas.

These include financial dealings (e.g. accumulating debts they cannot pay); behavior that puts others at risk (e.g. reckless or impaired driving, etc.); school behavior (e.g. failure to complete assignments, etc.); work behavior (e.g. careless or sloppy performance not attributed to lack of ability); fulfillment of treatment, court, or institutional obligations (e.g. failure to attend treatment); and relationships with family and friends (e.g. borrowing a friends property and damaging it).

16-FAILURE TO ACCEPT RESPONSIBILITY: unwilling to accept personal responsibility for their own actions (both criminal and noncriminal) or for the consequences of these actions. They usually have some excuse for behaviors that hurt others, including rationalization and placing the blame on others (e.g. society, the family, accomplices, victims, the system, etc.). In extreme cases, youth may deny accusations made against them, despite overwhelming evidence. For example there may be claims of being framed by others or of memory loss for the events in question. More frequently, though, individuals will accept responsibility for their actions in a superficial manner, and then will greatly minimize or even deny the consequences of these actions. Examples here include admitting to assaults, but claiming the victims lied about physical injuries, or admitting to thefts, but claiming that because the victims were insured, nobody really suffered.

17-UNSTABLE INTERPERSONAL RELATIONSHIPS: Individuals exhibit unstable, superficial and turbulent extrafamilial relationships, whether sexual or nonsexual. Such individuals may enter freely into relationships with others but are unwilling tor unable to maintain such relationships over long periods of time. These individual relationships may fail because of a lack of interest, effort, or commitment, or because of physical or emotional abusiveness.

18-SERIOUS CRIMINAL BEHAVIOR: These include charges and convictions for criminal offenses, as well as criminal acts committed but for which the individual has not been charged. Both the frequency and severity of criminal acts are considered.

19-SERIOUS VIOLATIONS OF CONDITIONAL RELEASE: Individuals who have committed 2 or more serious violations of conditional release or who have, on 2 or more occasions, escaped or attempted to escape from a secure institution. All types of conditional release are considered, including parole or mandatory supervision, probation, bail, and temporary absence or furloughs. Serious violations of conditional release are defined as 9a) those resulting in revocation of a conditional release or (b) engaging in criminal acts while on conditional release.

20-CRIMINAL VERSALITY: This describes the many different types of criminal behavior during their criminal careers (only include criminal behavior committed since age 11). Rather than specializing in crimes (e.g. property, drug, violent, and sexual offenses).

Traumatic Brain Injury

Be sure to ask about head injuries during the social history. More and more research tells us that even minor or mild appearing head injuries can have long lasting and complex negative effects of learning and behavior.

Mechanisms of Neuronal Damage from TBI
*Contusions
*Diffuse Axonal Injury
*Hematomas (Epidural, Subdural, Intracerebral)
*Cerebral Edema
*Hydrocephalus (Intracranial Pressure)
*Infection
*Neurotoxicity (Calcium influx, Excitotoxin release, Lipid peroxidation, phospholipase
        Activation)

Factors influencing outcome after TBI- (Aspin's Past)
*Anosmia   *Severity   *Psychiatric   *Intellectual   *Neurological *Sociopathy
*Premorbid behavior *Age   *Social   *Type of Injury

Personality Changes
*Labile type = affective lability: argumentativeness; isolative; disruptive; anxious
*Disinhibited type = poor impulse controls, i.e. sexual indiscretion, shop lifting, etc.
*Aggressive type = aggressive behavior; >behavior disorders suggest previous TBIs
*Apathetic type = marked apathy and indifference
*Paranoid type = suspiciousness or paranoid ideation
Other type = personality change associated with seizure disorder
*combined type = more than one of the above
*Unspecified type

Affected Executive Functions
*Setting Goals
*Assessing strengths and weaknesses
*Planning and directing activity
*Initiating and inhibiting behavior
*Monitoring current activity
*Evaluating results

TBI Severity Grade

(Mild=LOC<20";PTA= <24hrs)　　(Mod = LOC 20"-36hr; PTA=1-7days)
(Severe =LOC >36hr; PTA=. 7days)

Alt mental status	Characteristics	Pathophysiology
I- Confusion;	Norm consciousness w/o amnesia;	Cortical-subcortica disconnect(CSD)
II-Confus & Amnes;	Norm consc w/ confus & PTA;	CSD; poss. Diencephalic disconnect
III-Conf & Amnesia;	Norm consc w/conf, PTA & RGA	CSD & Diencephalic Disconnection(CSDD)
IV- Coma (Paralytic)	Conf w/PTA & RGA	CSDD & mesencephalic disconnect CSDMD)
V- Coma	Persistent veg state	CSDMD
VI- Death	Fatal Injury	CSDMD

RISK ASSESSMENT

These are great checklists that you can use when assessing a student for risk of violence.

Risk Assessment: Student Profile
A review of background information and student risk factors

1. Age at first school disciplinary referral_____
2. Number/type of disciplinary referrals_____
3. Number/type of suspensions_____
4. Number/type of expulsions._____
5. Degree of negative peer influence_____
6. Drug use_____
7. Incorrigible behavior at home_____
8. Number of runaways_____
9. Dx of ODD_____
10. Dx of ADHD_____
11. Hx of frequent geographical relocations._____
12. Placement in Foster Care._____
13. Hx of frequent changes in schools._____
14. Hx of domestic violence_____
15. Age at time of parental divorce_____
16. Involvement in excessive computer/video game use affecting sleep_____
17. Glib/superficial attitude_____
18. Grandiose sense of self worth_____
19. Lack of concern/remorse for inappropriate behavior_____
20. Manipulative behavior/con-man attitude_____
21. Shallow affect_____
22. Callous lack of empathy_____
23. Poor anger control/impulsive_____
24. Constantly blames others for problems_____
25. Does not accept personal responsibility_____
26. Unstable interpersonal relationships_____
27. Versatile juvenile delinquent acts_____
28. Cruel with pets/other people_____
29. Considered to be a bully/teases others_____
30. Depressed/Suicidal ideation/hx of gestures_____
31. Complains about being victim of teasing/bullying_____
32. Poor grades/learning disability/special ed_____
33. No special ed but slow learner/poor verbal skills_____
34. Peer rejection_____
35. Feels disrespected by others_____
36. Frequent fighting/aggressive_____

Risk Assessment:Protective Factors

1. Close relationship with parent(s)_____
2. Appears loving and affectionate_____
3. Shows concern for pets/other family members_____
4. Stable parental marital relationship_____
5. Few/no geographical relocations_____
6. Few/no changes in schools_____
7. Good/adequate grades/commitment to schooling_____
8. Stable neighborhood environment_____
9. Good peer group socialization skills and friendship making behaviors_____
10. Good verbal skills/communication skills_____
11. Good problem solving skills_____
12. No hx of juvenile delinquency_____
13. Cooperative/compliant with parental requests_____
14. Polite and respectful toward teachers/other adults_____
15. Good with pets/responsible/loving_____
16. Pleasant attitude towards others_____
17. Likes teachers_____
18. No hx of drug abuse_____
19. No hx of family dysfunction_____
20. Takes responsibility for behavior/consequences_____

INDEX OF FAMILY RISK FACTORS
"RUTTERS INDICATORS"(1985)

1. severe Marital Discord
2. low socioeconomic status
3. overcrowding/large family size
4. parental criminality
5. maternal psychopathology
6. placement of child outside of the home/foster care

Four or more risk indicators indicate a 21% increase in child psychopathology

Dyssemia
Stephen Nowicki,Ph.D. and Marshall Duke, Ph.D.

So, you are evaluating a student who may manifest signs and symptoms of Asperger's, Autism, or some other form of communication disorder with social deficits. **Dyssemia** is the difficulty with receptive and/or expressive nonverbal communication, and is an area of recent research that is both interesting and informative.

Dr.'s Norwicki and Duke have researched this topic and have written the book **"Helping the Child Who Does Not Fit In"**. An extremely interesting read and informative book.

Kids with communication and social interaction deficits may manifest Dyssemia. These deficits may be part of the autistic profile, but can also be associated with ADHD, social anxiety, and other conditions. **Dyssemia** is a difficulty with receptive and/or expressive nonverbal communication. The word comes from the Greek *dys* (difficulty) and *semia* (signal). The term was coined by psychologists Marshall Duke and Stephen Nowicki in their 1992 book, *"Helping The Child Who Doesn't Fit In"*, to decipher the hidden dimensions of social rejection.

These difficulties go beyond problems with body language and motor skills. Dyssemic persons exhibit difficulties with the acquisition and use of nonverbal cues in interpersonal relationships. "A classic set of studies by Albert Mehrabian showed that in face-to-face interactions, 55 percent of the emotional meaning of a message is expressed through facial, postural, and gestural means, and 38 percent of the emotional meaning is transmitted through the tone of voice. Only seven percent of the emotional meaning is actually expressed with words." Dyssemia represents the social dysfunction aspect of nonverbal learning disorder.

Jane E. Brody of the New York Times describes in the back cover of the Nowicki-Duke book[1] the sufferers of this condition: "We've all known children like this:
- they stand too close and touch us in annoying ways;
- they laugh too loud or at the wrong times;
- they make stupid or embarrassing remarks;
- they don't seem to get the message when given a broad hint or even told outright to behave differently;
- they mistake friendly actions for hostile ones, or vice versa;
- they move too slowly, or too fast, for everyone else;
- their facial expressions don't jibe with what they or others are saying, or
- their appearance is seriously out of step with current fashions, they don't dress well for the occasion, etc.
- they are known to stare at people, stalk people, or do something that annoys other people or make them feel uncomfortable
- they have problems dating and interacting with the opposite sex in a romantic way. Many dyssemics are love-shy."

Children with dyssemia fail to appropriately read (decode), and/or produce (encode), nonverbal communication or interpersonal information, the language of relationships, as asserted by Nowicki and Duke.

Dyssemic individuals exhibit problems with facial expressions, gestures, body posture, pitch and tone of voice, touch and interpersonal space, mood adaptive manners, punctuality, functioning, and performing in rhythm with the environment, clothing, make-up, and hairdo style.

Dyssemia sufferers tend to lack various skills indicative of emotional intelligence (EQ). Dyssemia is the nonverbal communication aspect of Nonverbal Learning disorders. More often than not, dyssemia concurs with developmental coordination disorder, a neurological aspect of nonverbal disorders consisting in a lack of coordination of body movements and mannerisms. Depending on the symptoms, dyssemia could be diagnosed as social anxiety or Communication Disorders Not Otherwise Specified.

Duke and Nowicki have developed a Dyssemia Rating Scale that is useful in many situations; and can be useful in determining if a child manifests those social deficits that ARE present in Autistic Spectrum Disorders (ASD); but just because a child scores high doesn't mean they have ASD. Be careful to note the additional characteristics that accompany Autism/Asperger's beyond the social and communication deficits.

People with Asperger syndrome often display **behavior, interests, and activities that are restricted and repetitive and are sometimes abnormally intense or focused.** They may stick to **inflexible routines, move in stereotyped and repetitive ways, or preoccupy themselves with parts of objects. Pursuit of specific and narrow areas of interest is one of the most striking features of AS.** Individuals with AS may collect volumes of detailed information on a relatively narrow topic such as weather data or star names, without necessarily having a genuine understanding of the broader topic. For example, a child might memorize camera model numbers while caring little about photography. This behavior is usually apparent by age 5 or 6.

Although these special interests may change from time to time, they typically become more unusual and narrowly focused, and often dominate social interaction so much that the entire family may become immersed. Because narrow topics often capture the interest of children, this symptom may go unrecognized.

Stereotyped and repetitive motor behaviors are a core part of the diagnosis of AS and other ASDs. They include hand movements such as flapping or twisting, and complex whole-body movements. These are typically repeated in longer bursts and look more voluntary or ritualistic than tics, which are usually faster, less rhythmical and less often symmetrical.

Dyssemia is considered a difference rather than a disability; as such, it is not classified as a standard medical condition. Many times dyssemia springs from cultural differences; other times, dyssemia constitutes an offshoot of ADHD. However, the differences can be devastating. Problems associated with dyssemia in the establishment and maintenance of interpersonal relationships are often at the root of people's social and occupational troubles.

Sometimes, persons affected with mild Asperger Syndrome or (AS) or social anxiety disorder also struggle with characteristics of dyssemia. Dyssemia can be remediated through a variety of programs designed to assess its presence and alter its adverse impact. Such programs, not unlike acculturation, emphasize virtual and social learning.

The Dyssemia Rating Scale (DRS) – School Screening
(Non-Verbal and Social Communication Deficit)

References:
Duke, M., Nowicki, S. and Martin, E.1996. Teaching Your Child the Language of Social Success. Peach Tree Publishers.
Nowicki, Stephen and Duke, Marshall. 1992. Helping the Child Who Doesn't Fit In. Peachtree Publishers.
Nowicki, Stephen and Duke, Marshall. 2002. Will I Ever Fit In? The Free Press.

Anxiety Disorders in Children and Adolescents

It has been my experience that I see more students with learning problems exhibiting significant anxiety. Those with school refusal behaviors certainly have a higher degree of anxiety disorders then even those with learning disabilities. This is anecdotal information from my perspective and experience, not necessarily statistically a fact.

I hope this article on OCD and anxiety disorders can be of help to you in your understanding of the various types of anxiety disorders and their impact on a student's academic performance.

What are anxiety disorders?

Anxiety disorders cause people to feel excessively frightened, distressed, and uneasy during situations in which most others would not experience these symptoms. Left untreated, these disorders can dramatically reduce productivity and significantly diminish an individual's quality of life. Anxiety disorders in children can lead to poor school attendance, low self-esteem, deficient interpersonal skills, alcohol abuse, and adjustment difficulty.

Anxiety disorders are the most common mental illnesses in America; they affect as many as one in 10 young people. Unfortunately, these disorders are often difficult to recognize, and many who suffer from them are either too ashamed to seek help or they fail to realize that these disorders can be treated effectively.

What are the most common anxiety disorders?

Panic Disorder -- Characterized by panic attacks, panic disorder results in sudden feelings of terror that strike repeatedly and without warning. Physical symptoms include chest pain, heart palpitations, shortness of breath, dizziness, abdominal discomfort, feelings of unreality, and fear of dying. Children and adolescents with this disorder may experience unrealistic worry, self- consciousness, and tension.

Obsessive-compulsive Disorder (OCD) -- OCD is characterized by repeated, intrusive, and unwanted thoughts (obsessions) and/or rituals that seem impossible to control (compulsions). Adolescents may be aware that their symptoms don't make sense and are excessive, but younger children may be distressed only when they are prevented from carrying out their compulsive habits. Compulsive behaviors often include counting, arranging and rearranging objects, and excessive hand washing.

Post-traumatic Stress Disorder -- Persistent symptoms of this disorder occur after experiencing a trauma such as abuse, natural disasters, or extreme violence. Symptoms include nightmares; flashbacks; the numbing of emotions; depression; feeling angry, irritable, and distracted; and being easily startled.

Phobias -- A phobia is a disabling and irrational fear of something that really poses little or no actual danger.

The fear leads to avoidance of objects or situations and can cause extreme feelings of terror, dread, and panic, which can substantially restrict one's life. "Specific" phobias center around particular objects (e.g., certain animals) or situations (e.g., heights or enclosed spaces). Common symptoms for children and adolescents with "social" phobia are hypersensitivity to criticism, difficulty being assertive, and low self-esteem.

Generalized Anxiety Disorder -- Chronic, exaggerated worry about everyday, routine life events and activities that lasts at least six months is indicative of generalized anxiety disorder. Children and adolescents with this disorder usually anticipate the worst and often complain of fatigue, tension, headaches, and nausea.

Other recognized anxiety disorders include: agoraphobia, acute stress disorder, anxiety disorder due to medical conditions (such as thyroid abnormalities), and substance-induced anxiety disorder (such as from too much caffeine).

Are there any known causes of anxiety disorders?

Although studies suggest that children and adolescents are more likely to have an anxiety disorder if their caregivers have anxiety disorders, it has not been shown whether biology or environment plays the greater role in the development of these disorders. **High levels of anxiety or excessive shyness in children aged six to eight may be indicators of a developing anxiety disorder.** Scientists at the National Institute of Mental Health and elsewhere have recently found that **some cases of obsessive-compulsive disorder occur following infection or exposure to streptococcus bacteria (Strep throat)**. This is referred to as **PANDAS.**

PANDAS, is an abbreviation for **Pediatric Autoimmune Neuropsychiatric Disorders Associated with Streptococcal Infections**. The term is used to describe a subset of children who have Obsessive Compulsive Disorder (OCD) and/or tic disorders such as Tourette Syndrome, and in whom symptoms worsen following strep infections such as **"Strep throat"** and **"Scarlet Fever"**. The **children usually have dramatic, "overnight" onset of symptoms, including motor or vocal tics, obsessions, and/or compulsions.** In addition to these symptoms, **children may also become moody, irritable or show concerns about separating from parents or loved ones. This abrupt onset is generally preceded by a Strep throat infection**. More research is being done to pinpoint who is at greatest risk, but this is another reason to treat strep throats seriously and promptly.

What treatments are available for anxiety disorders?

Effective treatments for anxiety disorders include medication, specific forms of psychotherapy (known as behavioral therapy and cognitive-behavioral therapy), family therapy, or a combination of these. Cognitive-behavioral treatment involves the young person's learning to deal with his or her fears by modifying the way he or she thinks and behaves by practicing new behaviors.

Ultimately, parents and caregivers should learn to be understanding and patient when dealing with children with anxiety disorders. Specific plans of care can often be developed, and the child or adolescent should be involved in the decision-making process whenever possible.

Section 504 has been updated and changed in accordance with ADAAA Jan. 1, 2009 changes

Americans with Disabilities Act Amendments Act of 2008 (ADAAA)

ADAAA Effective Jan.1, 2009

ADA Sec. 504. Read it. Understand it. Know it. It is a basic school law that every SSW must know in order to be effective in their support of those students with medical, physical, and mental impairments trying to survive in a large and complex the school environment.

SEC. 4. DISABILITY DEFINED AND RULES OF CONSTRUCTION.

"(1) DISABILITY.—The term 'disability' means, with respect to an individual—
"(A) a physical or mental impairment that substantially limits one or more major life activities of such individual;
"(B) a record of such an impairment; or
"(C) being regarded as having such an impairment (as described in paragraph (3)).
"(2) MAJOR LIFE ACTIVITIES.—
"(A) IN GENERAL.—For purposes of paragraph (1), major life activities include, but are not limited to, caring for oneself, performing manual tasks, seeing, hearing, eating, sleeping, walking, standing, lifting, bending, speaking, breathing, learning, reading, concentrating, thinking, communicating, and working.
"(B) MAJOR BODILY FUNCTIONS.—For purposes of paragraph (1), a major life activity also includes the operation of a major bodily function, including but not limited to, functions of the immune system, normal cell growth, digestive, bowel, bladder, neurological, brain, respiratory, circulatory, endocrine, and reproductive functions.
"(3) REGARDED AS HAVING SUCH AN IMPAIRMENT.—For purposes of paragraph (1)(C):
"(A) An individual meets the requirement of 'being regarded as having such an impairment' if the individual establishes that he or she has been subjected to an action prohibited under this Act because of an actual or perceived physical or mental impairment whether or not the impairment limits or is perceived to limit a major life activity.
"(B) Paragraph (1)(C) shall not apply to impairments that are transitory and minor. A transitory impairment is an impairment with an actual or expected duration of 6 months or less.
"(4) RULES OF CONSTRUCTION REGARDING THE DEFINITION OF DISABILITY.—The definition of 'disability' in paragraph (1) shall be construed in accordance with the following:
"(A) The definition of disability in this Act shall be construed in favor of broad coverage of individuals under this Act, to the maximum extent permitted by the terms of this Act.
"(B) The term 'substantially limits' shall be interpreted consistently with the findings and purposes of the ADA Amendments Act of 2008.
"(C) An impairment that substantially limits one major life activity need not limit other major life activities in order to be considered a disability.
"(D) An impairment that is episodic or in remission is a disability if it would substantially limit a major life activity when active.
"(E)(i) The determination of whether an impairment substantially limits a major life activity shall be made without regard to the ameliorative effects of mitigating measures such as—

"(I) medication, medical supplies, equipment, or appliances, low-vision devices (which do not include ordinary eyeglasses or contact lenses), prosthetics including limbs and devices, hearing aids and cochlear implants or other implantable hearing devices, mobility devices, or oxygen therapy equipment and supplies;

"(II) use of assistive technology;

"(III) reasonable accommodations or auxiliary aids or services; or

"(IV) learned behavioral or adaptive neurological modifications.

"(ii) The ameliorative effects of the mitigating measures of ordinary eyeglasses or contact lenses shall be considered in determining whether an impairment substantially limits a major life activity.

"(iii) As used in this subparagraph—

"(I) the term 'ordinary eyeglasses or contact lenses' means lenses that are intended to fully correct visual acuity or eliminate refractive error; and

"(II) the term 'low-vision devices' means devices that magnify, enhance, or otherwise augment a visual image.".

What is the expanded definition of "major life activities" under the ADAAA?Under the ADAAA, "major life activities" is expanded to include "major bodily functions." The statute contains a non-exhaustive list of "major life activities" that adds additional activities to those currently listed in the ADA and Section 503 regulations, and a non-exhaustive list of "major bodily functions." Specifically, the ADAAA provides that:

Major life activities include, but are not limited to, caring for oneself, performing manual tasks, seeing, hearing, eating, sleeping, walking, standing, lifting, bending, speaking, breathing, learning, reading, concentrating, thinking, communicating, and working.

Major Bodily Functions include, but are not limited to, functions of the immune system, normal cell growth, digestive, bowel, bladder, neurological, brain, respiratory, circulatory, endocrine, and reproductive functions.

What are "mitigating measures"?As used in the ADAAA, "mitigating measures" are things that lessen or ameliorate the effects of an impairment, including, but not limited to:

• medication, medical supplies, equipment, or appliances, low-vision devices (not including ordinary eyeglasses or contact lenses), prosthetics, including limbs and devices, hearing aids and cochlear implants, or other implantable hearing devices, mobility devices, or oxygen therapy equipment and supplies; use of assistive technology; reasonable accommodations or auxiliary aids or services; or learned behavioral or adaptive neurological modifications.

May the ameliorative effects of mitigating measures be taken into account when determining whether an impairment is substantially limiting?

No. With one exception, the ADAAA specifically prohibits consideration of the ameliorative effects of mitigating measures when assessing whether an impairment substantially limits a major life activity. This means, for example, that the ameliorative effects of the insulin or other medications a person uses must NOT be considered when determining whether that person's medical impairment is a disability. The one exception to this rule is the use of "ordinary eyeglasses or contact lenses.

" The ADAAA expressly requires consideration of the ameliorative effects of "ordinary eyeglasses or contact lenses" when assessing whether impairment substantially limits a major life activity. This means that when determining whether a person is substantially limited in the major life activity of seeing, the person's vision should be assessed in its corrected state when using such eyeglasses or contact lenses.

What to Consider Before Determining if a Student is Eligible
for
IDEA or 504 Services

1. Determine if the student is making reasonable academic progress in a regular education classroom and curriculum.

2. If yes, is the academic progress a result of the student's learning; or, is it because of teacher accommodations and interventions. Is the progress age appropriate and grade appropriate?

3. If the student is not making reasonable academic progress, has there been a Student Support Team meeting to define what, if any, educational supports and strategies may be useful in assisting the student to make reasonable progress in regular education classroom experience and curriculum.

4. Is there a positive or negative response to the Student Support Team's (SST) recommendations and interventions implemented by the regular education teacher?

5. If there is a lack of a reasonable response to academic interventions, does the regular education teacher suspect that some sort of learning disability may be adversely impacting the student's ability to make reasonable academic progress.

6. If someone suspects that one of the many types of learning disabilities may be the cause for the student's lack of progress, has the student been referred for evaluation by the 504 committee or SPED committee?

About the Author

DR. Raymond D. McCoy, Jr. BS, MSW, Psy.D. received his BS in Criminology from FSU in 1971; the MSW from FSU in 1977; and the Psy.D. from California Southern University in 2003.

He was a Licensed Clinical Social Worker from 1980 – 2014; and a Licensed Clinical Psychologist in California (Inactive-Out of State) from 2007 – present.

He has worked as a Juvenile Probation and Parole Officer; Social Security Disability Examiner; Child and Adolescent Mental Health Psychotherapist; Active Duty US Navy, (LCDR), Medical Service Corps, Social Work Department Head; Full Time and Part Time Private Practice LCSW; and School Social Worker for 21 years: Spanning a total of 43 years.

Every job he held prepared him to be a School Social Worker. The profession of School Social Work is so much more than just being a social worker in the schools. Any and all experience previously held will only add to your wisdom and clinical acumen required to be a proficient and effective professional School Social Worker.

Dr. McCoy retired in 2014 from active LCSW private practice and School Social Work.

He is now HAPPILY RETIRED!

Made in the USA
Coppell, TX
29 July 2021

59615931R00076